Decorative
Victorian
Glass

Front Cover
A late 6-way Stourbridge commercial epergne, about
1925. All features point to a carefully designed
specimen with clear lines to remove the impression of
an early Victorian style. The tops are turned instead
of frilled and even the brass fitting is the expensive
'crimp' of Birmingham, but it is still only an ornament.
58.4 cm (23 in) high.

DECORATIVE VICTORIAN GLASS

Cyril Manley

WARD LOCK LIMITED·LONDON

Dedicated to Rheola
for her patience and understanding
over fifty years

© Text Cyril Manley 1981
© Illustrations Ward Lock Limited 1981

First published in Great Britain in 1981 by
Ward Lock Limited, 47 Marylebone Lane,
London W1M 6AX, a Pentos Company.

Designed by Andrew Shoolbred
House editor Suzanne Kendall

Text filmset in Photina
by MS Filmsetting Limited, Frome, Somerset

Colour origination by Bridge Graphics
Limited, Hull

Printed and bound in Hong Kong by
South China Printing Company

British Library Cataloguing in Publication Data

Manley, Cyril
    Decorative Victorian glass.
    1. Glassware – Great Britain – History
    I. Title
    748.292   NK5143

ISBN 0-7063-5966-6

Contents

Acknowledgments

I wish to express my sincere thanks to the scores of people, both in and outside the glass trade whose patience I have tried for hours in lengthy discussions on glass and in seeking out information. In particular I am indebted to Stan Eveson, formerly Works Manager and Glass Technologist at Thomas Webb & Co. Ltd., and Tom Jones, Chief Designer at Stevens & Williams Ltd. Over many years both of them have never failed to help me with the many problems I have encountered. My thanks are also due to those Museums and Reference Libraries, in particular the Birmingham Reference Library, which have been a regular source of information.

But this book would not have been written had it not been for Miss Sadie Harris who insisted that it was needed and urged me to contact the publishers. The Editor, Miss Suzanne Kendall and Design Manager, Mr. Andrew Shoolbred have guided me through a maze of format intricacy and have made my task so much easier. I am greatly indebted to Clendon Walters for turning my hastily sketched drawings of trademarks into works of art, to Mr. Angelo Hornak for coping so magnificently with the tricky task of photographing the hundreds of examples chosen for the book, and to the typists who have had the difficult task of reading my writing.

Finally I wish to record my appreciation of the constant help and advice of my two sons and their wives.

Preface

As a dealer in antique glass for over thirty years, I remember that back in the 1950s Victoriana belonged to the market stalls of London's Portobello Road and not the showrooms of dealers of quality items. Twentieth-century sophisticates had contemptuously ignored all things Victorian and much had been carelessly discarded. But gradually people realized that the Victorians had produced some superb pieces of art, craft and manufacture. In the field of glass the growing interest caught many important dealers by surprise, for despite the large numbers of books on glass generally, little attention had been paid to Victorian art glass, leaving them unqualified to advise prospective buyers and would-be collectors. Cyril Manley has made it his life's work to collect and classify, research and painstakingly record the masterpieces of Victorian glass and in this authoritative book he is sharing his accumulated knowledge with all those who have learnt to appreciate the marvellous skills of the Victorian glassmakers.

Over the years I have had the good fortune of always being able to rely on Cyril Manley's willing advice and expertise and I therefore consider it a very special privilege to have been asked to write the preface for his book which I confidently predict will become a classic reference work. I am very pleased to have the opportunity of thanking him publicly for all the help he has given me and many others in our quest for more information about Victorian art glass.

Eric Lineham
London 1981

My purpose in writing this book

Over the past thirty years, literally hundreds of glass collectors and people who have shown a keen interest in Victorian glass, have visited my home to see my collection. Many of these visits have been accompanied by long discussions on how one identifies the myriad of types of glassware produced in Britain over the period, and I have almost always been asked to recommend a book or books where information on identification can be found. Although it is true that many books have been written on what has been termed this 'nonsensical period' of glass production, there is none, so far as I can discover, which will answer the sort of questions to which we are seeking answers.

Visitors have generally stated that they do not want a book which illustrates museum pieces. They want one which shows hundreds of specimens printed in colour with detailed descriptions of each, and these specimens must be of the type which they have discovered, and can still discover, whilst browsing in antique and second-hand shops. They want to have as many trademarks as possible in a book to help them identify their 'finds', and they want an easy reference guide for dating these from the Rd registration numbers. They are also generally interested in reading something about the glassworks where the products were made, with comments on the types and styles of glass produced by these 'works'. A number have expressed an interest in doing their own research.

Whilst I have, on many occasions, considered attempting to put my knowledge, such as it is, on paper, the task has always seemed too great. But now, in my eightieth year, I feel that I should do everything I can to help all those who are interested in glass of this period.

The Victorian era of glass production is probably the most difficult to comprehend and research. Those with the slightest knowledge of the period will understand this. But if I can throw any new light, give any additional knowledge whatever, or proffer any advice in helping to identify the products of our glassworks, then I shall have achieved my purpose.

This book, therefore, has been written to help the 'ordinary' glass collector – if any collector can be considered 'ordinary'. I cannot give all the answers for I don't know these myself – I wish I did. But if I can help to separate what some might term the 'rubbish' from the 'treasures' produced in the period, then possibly I shall have helped someone, somewhere.

Glossary

Acid polishing Today this term is used to refer to any matt-finished glass surface which is smooth polished by dipping it into a mixture of hydrofluoric and sulphuric acid. The Victorian period saw the commencement of using acids to save labour costs. By mixing a number of acids in very accurate percentages it was possible to polish, matt-finish or (and very important) to dissolve glass. It was this last process that made cameo commercially practicable.

Annealing During the manipulation of molten glass, terrific strains and stresses are produced if glass is allowed to cool quickly. To alleviate this, annealing is begun immediately the article is finished. The glass is placed on a conveyor which passes along a heated tunnel called a lehr. These lehrs were chiefly coal-fired in the Victorian period and the results were very unpredictable. Correct annealing needs to be very gradual to prevent formation strains.

Batch The raw materials of glass, including chemicals, ready for melting. See Metal.

Blank Strictly speaking all undecorated glass articles are blanks, but in the trade only an undecorated free-blown crystal vase, goblet, salt, etc., is a blank. If self-coloured, the name of the object is prefixed by the colour, such as ruby vase, if cased, it gets its full name, e.g., ruby-cased blank.

Blowing-iron An iron tube about 2 cm ($\frac{3}{4}$ in) in diameter and 1 m (3 ft) long, one end has a mouthpiece, the other a thin ring fitted which helps to retain the gathering.

Cameo In glass technology 'cameo' is a type of glassware which takes its name from a pattern in relief. The direct opposite is intaglio when the pattern is 'cut out' and the decoration is a lot less fine because the pattern must allow for a large cutting stone

to be used. Beware the risk of being sold intaglio for cameo, the latter being very expensive.

Casing An ambiguous expression used quite innocently, but which in certain circumstances does not reflect an article's true value.

Three words, cased, overlay and flashed all mean the same to many collectors not conversant with glassworkers' jargon. Glassworkers, however, never seem to use the word in the wrong sense. The difference between cased and overlay is technical, but to collectors and the retail trade cased glass is overlay when the decoration is mainly cutting with only a minimum of engraving. Cased is designed for cameo and engraved patterns when generally the colours and texture are softer than the casings used for overlay. For both types examples can be found with many casings.

Flashed glassware is totally different – it is a very thin coating of coloured glass giving the appearance of no more than a stain, but in Continental Europe it is called casing. In Britain it is used on lampshades and for various industrial purposes.

Chair The word has two meanings in the glasshouse. Firstly it is a chair where the gaffer sits to finish each object, its long flat arms allowing him to revolve glass fixed to the blowing-iron or punty-iron. The second interpretation of the word is the team of glassworkers required to produce any type of glassware. The number in a team varies but the average is five, i.e., the gaffer, servitor (who sometimes occupies the chair), footblower, sticker-up and taker-in. There can be a number of chairs, governed by the size of the glasshouse and the amount of work available.

Crimping In the glass trade the top of any article is either smooth or wavy. With the wavy specimen the form was dictated by

the tools the glassmaker possessed, but there was also a cast-iron floor gadget called a 'Bollifer' which was shaped to form certain designs on the top of any ductile glass article pressed on it. The glassmen themselves were using expressions such as crimped or 'scolloped' tops and in 1884 John Northwood patented what he called a 'crimping machine', not a machine in the strict sense of the word but a circular frame of adjustable blades to form innumerable crimps, another row of bars would undercut a crimped shape if the specimen was slightly turned.

Crystal The dictionary describes crystal glass as of a superior composition and manufacture – this is true, but still vague for our purposes. In the trade, crystal is divided into two classes, lead crystal with a lead content of up to thirty-five per cent, and mixtures without lead, such as the soda-lime group. To the layman, crystal is always clear, but coloured crystal was and is still made, a great percentage is self-coloured and transparent. To make it more confusing many collectors call crystal 'white glass' to distinguish it from coloured – for the general public the word crystal must remain, with or without lead, but white glass should *only* be used for opal or milk glass.

Cullet Any kind of waste crystal – rejects, pontil ends, in fact any pieces of clear glass found lying about – all are broken up, washed and cleaned. It is very important and accounts for forty per cent of each batch. It acts as a flux, and reduces the melting time considerably. A number of precautions have to be taken, for example, wine bowls and tumblers must be broken otherwise the cup-shaped pieces trap air in the mixture. It is inadvisable to mix lead crystal and soda-lime. Such is the importance of cullet that in 1886 John Northwood patented a method to dissolve iron scale from the glass collars of blowing-irons to prevent contamination. Coloured cullet is very different, self-coloured rejects can be used for the same mixture, but cullet from cased waste is thrown away.

Domed foot Used extensively in Germany during the mid-Victorian period, the French seem to have employed it earlier in a more elaborate form and London glasshouses used the shape for a few years in the early 1820s. A little before 1840 Richardson's of Wordsley used the shape in its plain form, similar to the Germans – see the snake jug **24**. After 1870 the dome gave way to a foot with a series of steps, at first glance it seems elaborate, but personally I think it sedate and have reason to believe it resembles the French pattern used a little before 1800. All these remarks refer to coloured specimens, not crystal ones.

Engraving This is a form of decoration which should be fully understood by all collectors, because in ninety per cent of British glassworks engraving means only one type and that is copper-wheel engraving. Nevertheless, the other types of engraving, such as line work, stippling, diamond point and drill decoration has generally been left to freelance artists whose work produced in the seventeenth and eighteenth centuries should be studied to help in the identification of Victorian glass. In my opinion first-class copper-wheel engraving far exceeds other methods both in skill and value.

Etching This is similar to the method used to produce commercial cameo. A pattern was scratched through a coating of bituminous paint (Brunswick Black) and then the article was plunged into a mixture of hydrofluoric and sulphuric acid. The acid would dissolve the unpainted glass to practically any depth. Unfortunately the acid etching of today is little more than a few thousandths of an inch deep and is not of much value unless signed by a prominent artist.

Fire polishing A method used to smooth out irregularities on a machine-pressed article immediately after the pressing process. All kinds of surface blemishes are common on pressed goods, but most can be removed by quickly re-heating at the furnace mouth, and this includes the mould fins which can develop because of excessive

use. Moulds have a limited life which is shortened if the surface decoration is intricate. The pattern can easily be blurred if the re-heating process is prolonged.

Flashing See Casing

Fleck A trade name for all small particles of any material used in the making of 'Aventurine' glassware. Powdered brass, copper and various minerals were all called mica-flecks. An example is 'Venetian' glass which appears to have in its mixture gold dust, but if this is so, as sometimes claimed, why doesn't it dissolve in the making?

Flint Another expression which refers to crystal, usually of very good quality.

Folded foot See Welted edge

Footblower or **footmaker** Second assistant, very important if blown feet are wanted (in wine glasses for instance) and can take over as servitor. See Chair.

Free-blown Here we have a contradiction in terms. Officially free-blown means without the aid of moulds but glass-blowers frequently use hollowed wooden blocks with a variety of curvatures and sizes. These rounding-up blocks, as they are called, are used after the first blowing to form and stabilize the base of any article before proceeding any further with the making – but they *are* moulds. This in no way belittles their skills, but it makes their job a little less frustrating.

Frigger or **whimsey** A term which always raises a smile when mentioned. It is a glass object made in a glasshouse generally frivolous, perhaps an apprentice piece, but sometimes serious, especially if it is an exceptional piece and leads to a new type of glassware. Actually, very few friggers were kept by the makers, most were given away, some were made only to expound an idea. However well-made a frigger may be, it is uncanny how an experienced glassmaker can recognize it as such. Somewhere in the making, an operation has been hurried, quite often the pontil has been left unfinished. A little-known fact is that for many years Richardson's of Wordsley employed a glassmaker whose sole job was to make any new idea in any colour available, all mixtures were recorded and specimens examined.

Gadget A tool used by glass-blowers to hold the foot of any article to allow work to continue on the body. It consists of a long tube, one end having three spring-clips or hooks, which spring over the edge of the foot, automatically gripping and centralizing the article. The shape of the clips varies and sometimes the formation as well, but the principle remains the same. There is another variation of the head, which has a groove for the stem and foot to slide into, this has a spring pad to press against the base of the foot and both types have a rod passing along the tube for the operator to release the clips.

Gaffer See Chair

Gathering A quantity of glass (mixture) taken from the pot by either a blowing-iron or punty-iron.

Glory-hole A separate furnace for re-heating articles during production. It is not at all popular and where the size of an article permits, glass-blowers reheat at the furnace mouth.

Hook A small hand tool used for positioning threads and other applied decorations by the gaffer.

Intaglio See Cameo

Knop See Merese

Lehr or **leer** A long heated tunnel, starting in the glasshouse and finishing in the dispatch department. The temperature is working-heat at the glasshouse end and room temperature at the outlet. See Annealing.

Marver A large cast-iron plate, machined flat and polished. After the glass-blower takes his gathering he 'marvers' or rolls the metal (mixture) on the plate into a workable shape prior to blowing. As well as compressing the metal he takes mental note of temperature, this may mean another visit to the furnace mouth to reheat – the working-heat is vital.

Matsu-No-Ke A design registered by Stevens & Williams in 1884 but which covers a style of Japanese decoration used in the latter part of the Victorian period 1870–1910 by a number of English glassmakers. It was a style which allowed them freedom of expression, an attribute necessary for applied branches, stems, flowers and leaves in many colours, all being wound round an article where a suitable gap appeared – see **60**.

Merese Both 'merese' and 'knop' are decorations and confused by the layman. Here again the trade dictates – a knop is always a knob, which can be used singly or in numbers, see **292**, a wine with nine knops forming a stem. A merese, like a knop, is generally applied to a stem, but there the similarity ends. A merese can be any shape or size, flattened, horizontal or vertical and can also be knurled or angled and is often used as a joint. Occasionally a merese is the focal point of a goblet's decoration, being engraved to match the bowl.

Metal Batch, mixture and metal are all terms used to describe glass under different circumstances. The batch (the ingredients of glass) is put into the pot. When it is molten it is a mixture and when it is being worked it becomes metal. In the glass trade metal is used in a dual form – when the glass is being worked and when being packed.

Mixture See Metal

Overlay See Casing

Pontil-mark After an article is broken off the punty-iron, a ragged edge is left on the base of the specimen. In many cases, if the projection does not interfere with the article standing firm, the pontil is left alone. Should it cause the article to rock or it is a quality piece, the pontil is ground away leaving a shallow indentation, and if the

glassware is a specimen piece or a special issue the ground pontil will be polished. Collectors should note these remarks as it was not common practice to grind out the pontil or polish the pontil-mark before 1800. Isolated cases obviously occurred but it is a date worth considering when other factors are present.

Pot A fire-clay receptacle fixed into a furnace which in turn contains the mixture.

Prunt Buttons of glass representing anything from raspberries (the most common shape) to lions' heads. Most of these decorations are made by glassmakers using their own tools and at times a glass-blower could be recognized by his prunts. The tool itself is about 15 cm (6 in) long, the diameter large enough to have the prunt cut out of one end. After applying the glass button, the glassworker presses the tool over it, leaving the shape standing proud.

Punty-iron or **rod** A long iron rod with a small ring welded about 2 cm ($\frac{3}{4}$ in) from one end which picks up the gathering to form the pontil. The pontil is pressed on to the centre of an article being blown ready for the gaffer to continue with the making, after the article is severed from the blowing-iron. Punty-irons are now tipped with stainless steel or anti-scale material, but previously minute particles of iron scale could be found embedded in the pontil of old goblets and wines.

Servitor First assistant to the gaffer, generally capable of finishing.

Sticker-up Assistant who attends to the cleaning of blowing- and punty-irons, the removal of old and dirty pontils and who

ensures that the gaffer and servitor are not kept waiting.

Taker-in Generally a young assistant who oversees the glass as it starts through the lehr.

Tools Simple and sensible – the principle of fashioning glass is perhaps much the same as five hundred years ago, but tools are being improved rapidly. The practice of tipping the blowing- and punty-irons to prevent scaling has cleared up many problems. Pucellas (procellas or spring-tongs) with and without wooden inserts for forming shapes, wooden pallets for steadying the article being shaped, a range of shears with shaped blades, a number of inside and outside callipers and scores of special gadgets now form a glassmaker's tool kit.

Welted or **foot edge** There are a number of expressions which many collectors find very confusing – one of great importance is 'folded foot'. I have heard collectors say that the Venetians folded the edges of their wine feet up and over, the English folded theirs down and under. This can be true, but when the wines are dated by this method, we are all on unsure ground. In the first place very few glassmakers say folded foot – their expression is welted edge, and that refers to the top or foot of any article. As for dates, I do not think glassworkers have ever ceased making welted edges – I am not saying that a welted edge on an early wine must be disregarded, but it must be taken in context with other features. Old wines do tend to have their edges flat and irregular in contrast with later ones with edges rounded and even.

Introduction

Let me begin by stating that what I term coloured Victorian decorative glass was made not only during the long period of time when that remarkable lady was on the throne (1837–1901) but for some years prior to her accession and for some fifty years after her death.

In my opinion, and some may disagree, the seeds of a new era of glass-making were sown in the 1820s, many new styles and types of decorative coloured glass flourished during her reign, and some of these were further developed until as recently as the late 1940s. But what was so different about this 'new' glassware, and why for me and so many others today, is it so fascinating?

It was a period, as its description implies, when colour was introduced in all its brilliance, when, as the century progressed, new colours in glass were formulated – blues, yellows, greens, reds, even browns, and these in all their many shades. It was a period when new shapes were introduced, some plain, but many that, today, are considered grotesque. It was also a period when applied decoration was recognized as an art, and when, it would seem, the smallest as well as the largest pieces of glass were produced. And this glass, some of lead, but mostly of a soda-lime base, was made with both a matt and a gloss finish.

The previous period of glass manufacture – the Regency period, was quite well defined. The magnificent crystal specimens made during that period were a credit to the English glassworkers. Toward the end of that period, however, a little self-colouring seemed acceptable, but at no time did any of our factories market the brilliant colours of the Victorian era.

The change, it seems, began around 1818–20, when a few firms produced specimens in opal, of classical design, decorated with both biblical and classical figures in monochrome. This type was continued until the turn of the century, although with different glass mixtures. One would need a very fertile imagination to presume that this style was the forerunner of the glass which I have collected over the past fifty years. For some reason, and that reason may be found in the influence from the continent of Europe, the brightly coloured amorphous articles which were soon to be produced, appeared almost overnight.

Before we progress, we must always remember that the coloured Victorian glass which I have studied, was never the main product of the glass industry of Britain. The production of cut, and to a lesser extent, engraved crystal, was, and still is, the life-blood of our industry. The manufacture of coloured glass, it seems, always brought problems, and so, in most of our factories it was a sideline to be tolerated. Nothing was allowed to interfere with the production of crystal. Even at the very height of its popularity, coloured decorative glass came second to crystal.

But it was a very interesting period, one of trial and error. New ideas abounded, many were tried and some that were successful were produced on a commercial scale. Some types of decorative pieces were made for years, but some, it would seem, for only a few weeks. Many firms failed to keep records of their production of various types and some even destroyed them, for they must have believed them to be of little value as both types and styles changed frequently. Researching this period, therefore, has not been easy, but now let me tell you how my hobby began and how I gleaned my knowledge.

As I remember, my interest in decorative glass originated in the early 1920s. I was then working as an engineer for the Britannic Manufacturing Company, The Platts, Amblecote, near Stourbridge, an area renowned for its expertise in glass. This newly-formed firm was housed in an old glassworks once owned by Thomas Webb, well-known glassmakers even today, and we there made small metal fittings for Midland glass firms.

It was at this time that I was able to watch glass-blowers and decorators at work. I was fascinated by their skill and artistry, their dexterity was something that was new to me. Even then, more than fifty years ago, it seemed that they belonged to an age that was fast disappearing. Among the glass that I saw was a pair of cased vases (see **1**) yellow over white on a topaz foot and decorated by Kny Brothers, Designers and Decorators, whose work was similar to that of the Northwood Brothers. It was intended, so I was told, that this type of vase would be sold in Woolworth's 3d and 6d stores ($1\frac{1}{4}$p and $2\frac{1}{2}$p) but this did not prove a feasible proposition, for the cost of production alone was six shillings (30p) each!

I bought these vases and so began my collection. I felt at the time that the glass trade would soon adopt a 'conveyor belt' system of production. The specimens that I would collect would never be made again.

My interest was never in their investment value. There was a great deal of glass of all types in the Stourbridge area, and as I recall, I searched for good examples of every type and style that had been made. Every piece that I bought, I attempted to research and record. My aim was to find out not only where it was made but, if it was possible, who made it. It was a relatively easy task if the specimen bore a signature, for there seemed an unwritten law that 'outworkers' signed their pieces. If a factory produced a special 'one-off' piece, then the artist was generally allowed to add his signature. If the piece of glass bore a trademark, then that was very helpful, but even then there could be some confusion, because I discovered registered trademarks, and also what I term 'adopted' trademarks, but more of this later.

Whilst research from the records and books on the subject has helped me considerably in identifying unmarked specimens, I have tended to depend a great deal on meeting and talking to old glassworkers in all parts of the country. Many I have invited to my home and have discussed glass-making with them into the early hours of the morning. But many I have visited in their homes, looking at pieces they owned, and also taking with me glass about which I needed more information. I have always been made welcome in private homes, as indeed I have been in glassworks generally. Records, such as some firms have, have been made available to me, and experienced glassmakers and technicians have been allowed to spend their time passing opinions, and searching for information on many pieces which seem 'unidentifiable'. Unerringly, they have been able to select foreign pieces which they have always seemed to despise.

As the years passed I decided that firstly I must identify my glass pieces by the region in which they were made – be it Stourbridge, Birmingham, London, Bristol, etc., – for most types and styles were regional and then I should always attempt to identify the makers in that region.

In this book I will attempt to pass on all the knowledge I have gained over the past five or six decades, knowledge which will help the collector to buy wisely. But I cannot emphasize enough the necessity for the collector to visit as many glassworks as he or she can and to watch the glassmakers and decorators at work. I have been made welcome at factories throughout Britain, and the experience I have gained has been invaluable.

Even after so long a period of time, I still have a great deal to learn and I have a number of pieces which I cannot identify for certain. I still spend most of my time talking with people who have information which helps me, and almost every day I seem to learn something that is important and exciting. Not all my opinions may be correct. My research methods may not seem acceptable to many for they are based on the experience of myself and others, and my handling of glass. I don't believe that anyone can be one hundred per cent certain in identifying some pieces, but if I can help any collector to identify some of the pieces he cannot be sure of, or lead him to buy more wisely in the future, then I shall have achieved something of value.

Identifying glass by country

The problems which arise in attempting to identify glass often seem insurmountable. They certainly seemed so at times to me, but I never gave up. Any information I gleaned, from whatever source, I noted down and always attempted to verify. Wherever an article is made, at home or abroad, some small characteristic or personal touch is incorporated in the article being made. In isolation this is unnoticed, but as it is always there, it eventually forms part of the article's composition. The collector, if he or she is to be proficient, should look for and remember these 'trifles'.

I hope that the collector will read my comments in this chapter while, at the same time, keeping an educated eye on the illustrated pieces and captions. Note the details discussed and apply them to your own specimens or possible future purchases. Please also note that when I mention Germany I am referring to all the former states of Germany – Bavaria Bohemia/ Czechoslovakia, Saxony, etc.

Manufacturing methods

We know that manufacturing methods have changed very little since the Victorian age and this helps us considerably with our identification problems. Let us consider what I feel are the most satisfactory and helpful guide-lines.

We must firstly separate Continental from British – Continental being the glass from all the countries on the continent of Europe. The vase, **54**, is a fair example to begin with as it is signed 'Made in Czechoslovakia'. Forget the threads and I will explain how the vase was made and then how it would have been made in Britain.

The vase is mould blown. (The moulds were generally made of cast iron or bronze.) The mould would have a cavity bored out by machine the exact shape and size as the vase. To release the vase the mould was made in two, three or four parts which could be separated from each other. A gathering of the metal would be taken on the blowing-iron and inserted into the mould. The glass-blower would blow and turn it at the same time, this shapes and removes the surplus glass formed by a badly fitting mould. The partly cooled vase is now severed from the blowing-iron and this can be done in a number of ways, but the finish is always a flat top, generally ground. After annealing, the vase is ready for inspection. The top has been ground flat because it is easily the cheapest way to remove the superfluous glass. The base or foot which is part of the overall shape is hollow, and generally does not have a pontil. If however it has, this has been added, only to give help later in applying some form of decoration, but this is unusual.

The orthodox British way to make this vase is totally different. It would be more expensive to manufacture and could not compete for price in the same market. The glassmaker would need a drawing or copy, as the Continental glassmaker needed a mould. He would take a gathering as before, start blowing and shaping towards the correct size, with the emphasis on the foot's shape and size. It is this part which has to be transferred to a punty-iron, and it would have a small amount of glass as a pontil. After centralizing the vase, it is sheared off the blowing-iron, leaving the article to have its final shaping, which includes rounding the top edge. I have left out the finer details for the moment as they have no bearing on what is the essential difference between the vases.

First we need to check the top of a vase. The Continental vase has a flat top, frequently ground and even if made the British way, it would be flattened rather than rounded.

We have just seen how important the finish on the top edge of a vase can be, but what of the neck formation? In **14**, note the out-of-proportion neck, which has a very small diameter as it leaves the body, and a wide, flared top. This is a typical French design. Whether the reader likes or dislikes the shape, it must be considered as a national characteristic.

Let us now consider the necks of a large percentage of Bohemian vases. In **21**, look closely because there are a number of English specimens on the same page to compare later. The neck and sweep to the rim are nicely balanced, but the curve finishes a little way before the edge of the rim, leaving it over-hanging a little, without support. Now this is an English reproduction of a Bohemian vase, and what I have just pointed out is not so pronounced as on an authentic one, but it can still be seen. The curve finishes before the edge, giving the impression of a thin disc. A few of the English necks and tops can now be compared, see **23**, **28** and **31**. By being made on a pontil, the sweep of the neck joins the rounded edge of the top, adding strength to the design and top.

We must always remember that there can be exceptions, but should not forget that during the Victorian period, the glassworkers were trained to design to suit the national taste.

We will continue to refer to the Bohemian-type vase, **21**, because it represents a type which has all the characteristics I wish to explain. It was with this type of vase that the German manufacturers at the Great Exhibition of 1851 thought they had reached the pinnacle of success, and with slight variations it has remained a standard vase. These vases, although they were mould blown, had a pontil applied – this was necessary because of the hand work needed to complete them. To begin with a mould and then transfer to a pontil for a vase of this description appears to be unnecessary, but not knowing what work had to be done to the piece after the pontil was set, it would be silly to speculate. Anyway, we can see the results and that is all we need to note at the present time.

Assuming the glass-blower has finished his part of the work, we have an opal over ruby vase without any decoration and a pontil on the centre of the foot. It is here that the collector must concentrate. With all these vases and also with a large percentage of other German glassware, the pontil was ground off with a grinding wheel which left the surface absolutely flat, and in some cases it was also polished. Should there be a small indentation in the centre of the base do not be confused. This is because the operator has removed too much metal when first grinding off the pontil. Looking through the hollow base towards a light it will be seen to form an integral part of the shape.

The Bohemian hollow foot has a very strong following on the Continent, and it was not only confined to small and medium pieces. In fact their 30–60 cm (12–24 in) cased specimens (opal over ruby, opal over crystal, etc.) are very much sought after as works of art and most have hollow bases.

This is perhaps the appropriate time to draw the attention of the collector to the phrase 'opal over ruby'. This is how this particular vase would be described, and it is accurate. If a British glassmaker used this expression about his own glassware, he would mean opal (white) over a ruby glass blank, but to a German it can mean opal over a crystal blank stained red (in Britain this is called flashed glassware) and this is what most of the German vases are.

Before we leave the base of this vase, take particular note of the diameter of the foot, which, from a British point of view, is too small for the design.

We will now remark on the British foot. Whenever possible it was made solid. The servitor could make a foot at the same time as he fixed the pontil and in fact it was generally done that way. If because of design it had to be mould blown, the maker would compress it, making it solid. Alternatively, the article would be moulded and a separate foot added. Compared to the Bohemian foot, the British glassmaker would increase the diameter to approximately the size of the top.

The collector, however, must not assume that all vases with hollow bases are Continental. The British did make them, but there was always a specific reason, and the experienced collector must always look for this. The tall green vase, **31**, cased opal over green, is a fine example to show off a British blown foot, a foot that is hollow, but which nevertheless can have strength for a number of reasons. It is blown separately and cased, opal over green to match the rest of the vase. It is compressed when applied and centred, the casing doubles the strength. Even the cutting (decoration) is kept to a minimum to preserve that strength. In order to balance its height, the diameter of the foot is fairly large. It is made on a pontil which is then, generally, ground out.

Pinched feet, too, show a national characteristic. On a British vase they would be formed from an applied strip, the pontil adhering to the bottom of the vase, clear of the feet – the Continental version would cover the base of the vase completely.

Shape

Learning to assign a shape to a particular country is problematical to say the least. I used to attribute this skill to experience, but I have noticed that many people acquire the ability very quickly. Actually there are no hard and fast rules by which one can say that certain countries made use of definite shapes, but it might surprise many to find (if they are observant) that certain shapes, or combination of shapes, occur more frequently from some countries.

Over the years I have found that shapes reflect the 'feelings' of designers for that part of the world in which they spend most of their lives, and this can include shapes of anything around them. Compare specimens of glass from Sweden, Italy and Spain and you will see for yourself the difference in shapes. Most of the Italian and Spanish glassware are so 'foreign' that I feel we need not discuss them. Scandinavian glassware is very different in shape and was not made in any quantity until the early twentieth century and thus had no influence in the Victorian period.

From personal experience I have seen and heard what happened when Continental artists and glass-workers came to work in British factories. It sometimes took them years 'to settle' – we must remember that they were making articles with which they were unfamiliar and, more especially, working on unfamiliar shapes. This also happened in reverse when British glassmakers tried to copy certain German shapes.

British shapes are invariably plain and simple. A barrel is a good example, a shape which can take slight modifications without altering stability. A series of curves which form a pleasing outline when joined was also used. The collector will notice that the same curves occur frequently in both convex and concave shapes. Never, to my knowledge, do they double back when forming the general outline. The only sudden alteration of shape takes place at the top, and then only in the decorative sense.

Shapes and types

Can we associate a definite shape to a definite type? In theory yes, but in practice no. This is because of production methods. Basically each type of glassware has a special mixture and in certain circumstances this can govern the numbers produced.

Few people collecting glass know the conditions prevailing at the time when their treasures were produced. The first and most important factor was that whatever was made had to be sold. Also that a minimum number of articles had to be made from a pot of metal. These factors often decided the number, size, and also weight of the product. If, after the first few had been blown, it seemed likely that the number which

could be made from the pot was too small, the shape and thickness would be modified. If on the other hand, the glassmaker had metal left over after making the quota, all sorts of articles could have been made, some of which might go into production later. In fact, on some days many experimental pieces were produced.

The shapes of crystal tableware, which in many cases are registered, can be ignored, although occasionally these shapes also appear in ornamental specimens. I have often heard people at auctions and fairs say they knew what a certain piece of glass was and where it was made. On one occasion the piece was a specimen of Webb's 'Bronze', and the auctioneer stated that he knew the shape. This is something the collector must be wary of. In this case he was right, for it was made by Webb's, but the shape was copied from an excavated Roman vessel and Webb's had combined an unusual colour with the shape. It was the shape *and* colour which the auctioneer knew, not the shape alone. There are a few instances like this, and when it occurs, the collector must realize that these shapes are not necessarily used for any of the firm's other glassware.

We also have the case of a firm producing an exclusive type of glassware. We can be certain that after a few had been made, other shapes would have followed in the same glassware.

I mentioned the question of shape to a Director of a glass firm, and he stated that his firm had at least 80,000 shapes which could be used either singly or collectively on any type of their glassware and this was so with a large number of glassworks. I feel, therefore, that we must remember that shape alone cannot identify a firm's glassware.

To attempt to give a detailed description of all the shapes used in each country of Europe is an enormous task, far beyond my capabilities, and in fact I do not think it necessary. What we, as collectors of specifically British glass need, is sufficient knowledge to recognize Britain's own glassware. It is the glass from Germany and France which provide the difficulties, and we must remember that some of their craftsmen moved to Britain bringing with them their ideas which influenced British styles. Fortunately much of what they were responsible for is easily detected .

German glass

Germany will be considered first, as it is that country's products which were exported to Britain in the greatest number.

The obvious starting point is to compare and separate by shape. I have explained many of the British principles, so let us see how these contrast with those of Germany. To do this, it will help if we know something of the background history. Germany had an established glass-producing industry for many years before Britain and during the Victorian period developed a great export trade to many countries.

It was about 1820, as previously stated, that the British people began to show an interest in a more colourful type of glassware than the sedate crystal of the Regency period. Our manufacturers responded immediately, some with self-coloured articles suitably decorated, others with articles made entirely from coloured glass, chiefly ornaments. So the Germans, although with a thriving industry, making glass that was superb but expensive to produce, and well-established in the British market, could not compete for price with the home manufacturers whose transport costs were small. To compete in Britain, German manufacturers had to produce a totally different type of glassware.

Most collectors after a few years, will realize the similarities between the German and British types, and much of this was obviously intentional. They had to try to improve their export products and, more important, these had to be cheap. At this stage the Germans had to eliminate as much hand work as possible, and this led to a great many mould-produced articles. The result was that they produced some magnificent specimens for their own market, and an entirely different type of glassware for export. If we correlate our facts, we shall find little difficulty in separating German glass from British. The increased use of the mould allowed the Germans to make elaborate and unlimited shapes by the hundred and it is the elaborate shapes which characterize much Continental glass, so out of character with British glassware.

A quick test to decide mould-blown articles is to put two together. If they are exactly the same, with or without pontils, count them as Continental until further proof is available. The Germans also had to add colour to their glassware, again to compete. This is also helpful to collectors, for their colours are very gaudy and sometimes include black, which we rarely used, and gaudy colours are very uncommon on glass made in Britain.

So, by the end of the nineteenth century, the Germans were making two distinct types of coloured glassware. The one we will call 'Export', the other a 'National' type. The latter had shape and substance and had been established over the years, created by the character of the people. In many ways the shapes are similar to the British, but there the similarity ends, for the types and methods of decoration are so different, that after very little experience most collectors recognize them immediately. We will discuss their characteristics and also their differences from other countries later.

French glass

French glass was exported to Britain, but not in the quantities which we had from Germany. Neither did they make any alteration in their styles and types to improve their sales. Their specimens may prove more difficult to separate, but with some experience it can be done. (I leave out French-cameo which is so very different from English-cameo. Should a collector be interested and want advice in this field there is only one way to get it, see both kinds by visiting exhibitions and auction rooms and, if at all possible, handling these articles.)

Vases, centre-pieces and dressing table trinket sets from France will be the chief articles to interest collectors. The shape of vases and centre-pieces is our first consideration. They are in no way flamboyant, in fact they follow British shapes very closely, too close for collectors to be definite unless they are well-experienced. Very often it is a combination of the decoration and shape which decides the provenance. For shapes alone, I use a method which is purely personal. In my judgment most French vases appear top heavy, but let me hasten to clarify this statement. The top and base diameters and height never seem to harmonize, in my opinion, but in practice they are perfectly stable. Other collectors might well disagree with me, but for me it is a guide in identification. Whilst on the question of shape, and this applies chiefly to jugs, and French in particular, the shape of the top and spout are important. It is a shape referred to as the 'Shamrock' top. The shape is exactly what the word implies – one leaf is curled to form a spout, the other two are slightly twisted, and this has remained a common feature of French jugs. The British copied it frequently in the 1820s, but since it became used for crystal-ware, it lost its identity. In any case the collector will not be troubled with it very much in coloured ornamental glassware, as both French and British settled on a simple triform shape for jugs and vases.

Decoration

The styles of decoration used by the French help to identify their own glassware, exactly as those chosen by the Germans help to identify theirs. The importance of decoration has been mentioned before, but I do not apologize when repeating to the collector that he should pay very careful attention to it. A general rule is that first-class decoration will always be applied to a good, carefully designed and coloured article. In hundreds of cases the articles are designed to emphasize the decoration, in others, the shape, colour, and decoration are such, that at first glance we know we are seeing a first-class specimen. This, of course, is perfection and, naturally these pieces are not plentiful.

I will quote a very common occurrence. Think of the times we have seen a pair of vases decorated with a few insipid flowers and leaves. Unless they have been painted by an amateur after the vases were sold, the glass is of little consequence. This can easily be proved by trying to scrape off the paint – if it can be removed then the vases are second rate.

Until one becomes involved with glass, one's idea of decoration is confined to painting, enamelling and gilding, but those who do start collecting, soon realize they are in a completely new world. Techniques they had never heard of, have, in some cases, been developed solely for glass.

Some of the methods in common use are painting, enamelling, gilding, engraving, cutting, acid etching, and sand blasting. All have 'off-shoots' which in many cases rival a well-established operation. Enamelling is very complex, and if well understood helps to identify many specimens. First-class enamellers are always gilders, so on many articles one finds enamelling and gilding in the same design. However, gilding if cleaned frequently, has a very short life. This is decided by the type of base which all gold work should have, and also the method of firing (fixing). A lot of experimentation has been carried out to find a permanent base, but at the moment none is successful. If the specimen is only dusted and kept in a cabinet, we may use the word 'permanent' when referring to it. Different types of enamelling help to locate the country of origin or at least an artist's nationality, whether or not he was working in his native country. In my opinion if enamelling and gilding is studied closely, glass identification is made easier and more definite. Here I can only speak from experience, and when associating a decoration with a country I will try to elaborate.

My experience has shown that in attempting to identify British glassware, the difficulties again come mainly from the two countries, Germany and France. We have already examined the glass from both of these, so if we can find a little more information, it should strengthen our confidence. Let us look more closely at types of decoration.

I will first consider the German 'Export' type. The surface of a vase must be our first objective, being mould blown and, knowing the article is turned at the time of making, the specimen must be round. If any irregular shape or pattern was required, the mould would, when opened, leave a mould split projection which would require another operation to remove it, and this would increase the cost. (A similar operation was necessary for machine-pressed articles from our Northern region.) Cost would not allow much to be spent on applied decoration, possibly a flower and a leaf or two, in very watery colours. If handles were applied, they were generally malformed and thin, similar to those made in Italy (Venice). At one period, a few years prior to 1914, a series of similar shapes were made, a little better in workmanship, but both kinds were very light in weight.

What we have called the German 'National' type are really fine specimens. Most are heavy, much heavier than a similar British product. The foot is solid and thick, 19 mm ($\frac{3}{4}$ in) in some specimens, and they are often cut under the foot, not often with a star, but with deep cuts in squares and deep cuts at right angles, the cuts continuing down the edge of the foot. At times the top face of the foot, the stem and lower part of the vase or goblet is faceted, but there is always plenty of metal to spare. The cased ware is heavy, but they also used coloured stains (instead of casing) which I dislike.

Engraving is extensively used on most of the specimens, crystal, cased and stained, some of the engraving being 5 mm ($\frac{3}{16}$ in) deep. I know of no other country in the world which produced similar specimens in quantity. My advice to all collectors, if they are not familiar with this type of glassware, is to make an effort, however inconvenient, to see some.

With French glassware the collector is faced with something very different. Whereas the differences which we have noted with German export specimens are generally basic, those with French glass are not obvious, in fact decoration is very often the deciding factor. Here again it is sometimes part of a manufacturing technique.

In my opinion French enamelling can be put into

three distinct and easily recognizable classes. One is when the enamels are applied very thickly on large or small articles. Whatever the size of the article, colours are always bright and rounded, very stereotyped, and having the appearance of being mechanically applied. The second type could not be more different, colours thin and shaded, more in the manner of a water-colour, and floral designs are very realistic. It is this method of colouring which is frequently used on many of their cameo specimens, but the application and appearance is more rugged. On the third type, and again I use a floral design as an example, flower and foliage are more true to life than those on the German 'Export' issue.

French-cameo, as I have already stated, we will ignore because the only British glassware to compare it with is English-cameo, with differences so obvious that the collector has only to glance at one specimen of each kind to remember those differences. On reflection, there was, during the period of English commercial cameo a tendency on the part of French manufacturers to produce some of their own pieces using our methods. With these specimens anyone interested must have a very good knowledge of certain glass manufacturing techniques to separate French from the English, and separated they must be, because of the price each

commands. Generally, English-cameo art pieces will always fetch a higher price than French-cameo – unless the French example is a signed piece by Gallé.

To my knowledge, a type of pseudo-cameo vase has been around Britain for fifty years. It is shaped like an Indian club, the handle end having a flared top. It is very heavy and the wall of the vase is extremely thick. Around the surface is a decoration of raised flowers and leaves beautifully enamelled, but the glass-blower would require mechanical assistance to create a very clear-cut design. It was transferred to a pontil to have the top flared. The base is ground and polished in the Continental manner. I have seen scores of these vases, sold always as French and I have little doubt that they are French, yet when Richardson's sold out in the 1930s, a number of these vases, in various shapes and sizes, were found in the glasshouse.

Glass production in France was not confined to free-blown varieties. Their production of machine-pressed articles was quite extensive, some of the articles being similar to those of Britain's Northern region. My impression is that they were more functional than decorative, and were more plentiful in the latter part of the Victorian period. Signatures most often seen are Vallerysthal and Portieuse.

Identifying British glass by region

As previously stated, my primary objective was always to determine from which region of the British Isles any piece of decorative glass originated. I soon learnt how to distinguish 'foreign' specimens, for most of the glassworkers with whom I talked, were always keen to point out the differences not only in the style of glass, but also in the manufacture. And neither did it eventually prove too difficult to decide, approximately, the origin of the glass made in this country. Of course there were, and still are, the 'difficult' pieces, but more about those later.

I had always mentally divided Britain, for identification purposes, into the following regions. First and foremost, probably because it was on my own doorstep, was that of Stourbridge, which included Brierley Hill, Dudley and even Bromsgrove.

Second, was the Birmingham region, geographically only a short distance from Stourbridge, but where decorative glass that was 'different' was produced within a radius of only three kilometres (two miles) of the city centre. Glassworks in the London region also produced both different styles and types, whilst the glass produced in the Northern counties differed so much that I was soon able to determine whether it was made in the Manchester area (including St. Helens and Warrington) or the towns nearer to Newcastle-upon-Tyne, namely South Shields, Sunderland and Gateshead. The fifth region, as far as I was concerned, was that of Scotland.

Where, it might be asked, did Bristol fit into my scheme? As far as I can discover, no coloured glass worth collecting was produced there in the Victorian period. The well-known Bristol blue and white (opal), and the Nailsea style had been introduced in the eighteenth century, but by the 1820s, both Powell and Chance, whose factories had been the most important, had closed their gates, Powell taking over Whitefriars, and Chance moving to Smethwick, making mostly crown glass. Ricketts continued until 1833 making cut and engraved crystal, with some coloured ware.

Before I attempt to describe the styles and types made in these regions, it is important that the reader should be aware that in the glass trade itself, the terms 'Smooth' and 'Fancy' were generally used. Smooth glass was what one might expect – it did not have any projections and was smooth to the touch. It was generally made by the larger firms and always considered to be of better quality than fancy which was usually more colourful, and referred to as 'wake' or 'fair' glass. Although it was also made by the larger firms, a great deal of fancy was produced in small cribs, one-man or small family businesses. Great skill was needed in its production even though it was relatively cheap to buy. Records show that fancy glass was being made by the mid-nineteenth century, smooth in the late 1820s.

The Stourbridge area produced glass of nearly every style and type, both smooth and fancy. Of course, as most people are aware, it was the centre for cameo, but its factories also excelled in the production of applied decorative glass. Whether any machine-pressed glass was ever produced there is debatable – although there is some evidence of this, it was certainly not made on a large scale.

Some pressed glass was made in Birmingham, but most of that area's production was of the smooth style, as was that of the London firms. Much of the glass produced in London, however, was second class, except for the art pieces of the small firms of 'Gray-Stan' and Varnish and Company, and those of the well-known firm of Whitefriars.

The Manchester region was responsible for much 'functional' coloured glass, but its fancy ware was similar to that of the Stourbridge region. It was, however, the home of machine-pressed ware, as was the area around Newcastle, which was also the centre for slag.

In Scotland very little glass of note was produced, except at Alloa. Most Scottish glass was crystal, cut and engraved, except for Clutha, and later Monart.

The Stourbridge region

The Stourbridge area has been recognized as an important glass centre since the seventeenth century, but during the nineteenth and early twentieth centuries the workmen there exceeded all expectations and the area ranked as Britain's leading area for blown glass. Although its workers were familiar with all the then-known techniques, it was isolated, which demanded inventiveness on the part of the makers and artists. They needed, and they had, above-average skills with a determination to produce the best, and most of them, whatever their skill in the glass-trade, had spent some years at Richardson & Webb.

In 1836 Thomas Webb withdrew from the partnership and it was this separation which, in my opinion, allowed the Richardson group to produce the types of glass they wanted. The ten years before this date had been spent in getting together all methods of glass production and glass decoration under one roof. Under such conditions how could they fail? The firm then traded as W. H. & B. Richardson.

After leaving the Richardson & Webb partnership, Thomas Webb started up his own glassworks at The Platts, Amblecote in 1837, but his record suggests he had a very strong streak of individualism and was best working alone. He finally settled at Dennis Park where he built the original works in 1856 and there he prospered, producing both crystal and coloured. His crystal was good, neither better nor worse than any of the other glassworks of the time, but the individual coloured ware was to become famous. The cameo boom came after his death in 1869, but his son, Wilkes, backed it with all the factory's resources, and if that was insufficient he engaged outside specialists.

I never intended to write anyone's biography but mention of two men, John Northwood and Joseph Locke, will crop up time and time again, for they influenced both the English and American glass fashions.

John Northwood created or dominated many different styles and types and, by so doing, fixed positive dates, essential for identifying purposes. With the types and dates established, the collector can get to within two or three years of his specimens.

John and his brother Joseph had started a decorating business in 1860 and within ten years they were established with satisfied customers as far away as North Staffordshire. One very good customer was Stevens & Williams, and its Chairman, Mr. Joseph

Silvers Williams, offered John the position of Art Director. He accepted this in about 1880. A lot of discussion about design and development had been simmering for a few years previously as also had been the use of colour. These had to be used in the most artistic and commercial ways, so one important date for collectors to remember is 1880.

In glassware, as with other commodities, public fashion governs styles, and about this date 'fancy' ornaments were popular.

The first ornamentation was applied threads. Hand-applied threads had been used for hundreds of years as a decoration, but now it had to be applied mechanically and under control. This was achieved with a machine patented by John Northwood. The threads can be of any diameter, but 0.8 mm ($\frac{1}{32}$ in) seems to have been the one in general use.

We will leave threads for the present, because at the same time other types of decoration were being used in the fancy period. The most popular was 'applied' decoration consisting of leaves, flowers, reptiles – in fact, you name it, the glassworkers applied it! All kinds of leaves were being used and really without much thought. It seems that the acanthus leaf was agreed upon for the first commercial pieces.

During the same period, another glassworks, Boulton & Mills, Audnam Glass Works, operating less than two kilometres (one mile) away, had been using the acanthus leaf as a decoration for some time. In some cases their colours coincided with those of Stevens & Williams. This was of no concern to either company as copying or making a similar article did not matter, but to a collector today it raises problems of identification.

About this time the formation of applied flowers also underwent reappraisal, both for kind and method of application. The previous floral decoration had been made and applied in one of two ways. Firstly the flowers were made by hand with a lamp (lamp work) and in this way minute detail could easily be achieved, these flowers would be kept hot and applied to the heated body as needed. The second method was to place a small gathering of glass where the flower was wanted and then, using a flower prunt, press on a flower shape. Both these methods were in general use throughout the country.

The result of these deliberations was that a number of flower moulds were made and patented from 1881. The flowers from these moulds were kept heated and used when required. At the same time there was experimentation with colours, some of which were accidental, for details of the colour combinations of this period see page 35 and **126**.

John Northwood had two jobs. He had his own decorating business (which survived until the 1920s) and was Art Director to Stevens & Williams. He had been carving cameo 'on and off' for ten years, and during this time had been watched by the designers, engravers and management of most glassworks. In fact, many were trying to iron out the problems of cameo and speed up its production. It was obvious that 'cameo' had a future. The carving of the replica of the Portland Vase established John Northwood as a great artist, but we must not forget that there were others equally as good. With hindsight, it seems that it was only the time factor which deterred all but he – carving glass with primitive tools took time.

The answer to this problem of time came with the use of acid. Richardson's had worked with acids for years, in fact they had a permanent trade supplying goods decorated with patterns which were acid etched. With acid-etching the decoration was only surface thin, it had no depth and what was wanted now was greater depth. Increased depth needed engravers to tidy the pattern edges, and John Northwood employed many of the skilled men. How or why it happened, we do not know exactly, but his engravers moved to neighbouring glassworks, chiefly Thomas Webb and Stevens & Williams. Richardson's had their own engraving department, headed by Joseph Locke and he, with the firm's backing, started on the second replica of the Portland Vase. It was entered in the Paris Exhibition of 1878, without actually being finished. So by that date, with a combination of carving and acids, he had taken less than eight months to make it. The 'cameo' epoch was to last at least twenty-five years, during which time some magnificent art specimens and many commercial ones were produced.

Frederick Carder was chief designer at Stevens & Williams and saw the twilight of the 'fancy' period and the beginning of another 'smooth' period. In 1903, shortly after John's death, he abruptly left for America and John Northwood II followed his father as Art Director.

Is it possible for the collector to separate Northwood's glass from Carder's? My opinion is that Carder never made any 'fancy' in England. Perhaps he disliked the style for even in America there is little evidence of his making any. He was certainly designing for the 'smooth' period before he went to America, and he seems to have continued there. Some of his types use the same name as those in England but are different in many ways. The difference, of course, may have been intentional.

Mills, Walker & Co., Albert Glass Works, Bridge Street, Wordsley, 1884–95, is relatively unknown from a collector's point of view. It is known that Frederick Stuart was established at the works in 1856, with R. Mills, and he seems to have been the guiding genius because of his previous work on coloured glass. He left in 1881 to control the Red House Glass Works, Stuart's present works. After his departure, partners changed until finally it became Mills Walker & Co. in 1884. Very little fancy or smooth ware is known to have been made there but the specimen illustrated, **127**, is a treasure for a number of reasons. Being genuine it proves that firms other than Richardson and G. Bacchus of Birmingham produced 'Vitrified'.

Situated between Richardson's and Thomas Webb was the old-established firm of Boulton & Mills, Audnam Glass Works, Stourbridge, 1716–1926. The owners of this glass factory changed many times but eventually they settled down as Boulton & Mills when the factory was re-built and re-organized. Some authorities give that date as 1856, others as 1876. These dates, strangely enough, coincide with Stevens & Williams's 'fancy' period and their applied work. Some of the articles produced by both firms are so much alike that it took me years to discover how to separate them. I finally achieved it by using ultraviolet light.

Webb–Corbett, Coalbourn Hill Glass Works, Stourbridge, only a short distance from Thomas Webb & Sons Ltd., Dennis Glass Works, started officially as Webb & Corbett at the Whitehouse Glass Works, Wordsley in 1897. Prior to that date practically every Stourbridge glass personality had either owned it or worked there (it is here that the spiderweb trademark is supposed to have originated). In 1908 they moved to their present site, their output being crystal, and also cased ware in a number of colours. Their contribution to coloured Victorian glass was not extensive, but they did employ two good artists, Hugo Maisey as an employee and Jules Barbe, as an outworker.

Maisey (spelt in a number of ways) was a Bohemian artist greatly underrated. His enamelling is easily recognized because of its matt finish. Jules Barbe, perhaps the best of gold workers to come to Britain from France, was also a great enamel artist and he did most of their gilding. As far as Victorian coloured glass is concerned, the collector's period for Webb–Corbett is 1897–1946.

Details of a glasshouse trading as S. Edwards, Professional Glass-Maker, Gladstone Road, Wollaston, Stourbridge, have proved very difficult to find, but glass made there has been easy to locate. A cone which was supposed to be part of that glassworks was demolished in 1900.

The 'Heath' Glassworks was situated where Mary Stevens Park is now. Whilst a great deal is known about the works, very little has been discovered of the glass made there. It was established around 1600 and is thought to have been one of the earliest works in Stourbridge. What type of glass was made there between 1860–82? (The last date is when, it is thought, production ceased.) It was considered to be 'Continental rubbish' by Midland dealers for many years and still is, by most junk merchants. I agree that it looks poor until examined by someone with glass-making knowledge. The characteristics of making, common in Stourbridge early in the nineteenth century, together with the large amount in shops caused me to study the pieces more closely, for an example see **167**.

After some time I found a family whose grandparents had worked at the 'Heath'. To add to my earlier evidence their house contained scores of different pieces. Included in the glass I have examined are wines and decanters of crystal and what appears to be ruby over crystal or possibly a very thick stain. Obviously they made many other types of glassware but there is evidence only of chandeliers, fairly common in the area.

Very little research has been accomplished on Harrop, Hammond & Co. Ltd., Harts Hill Glass Works, Vine Street, Brierley Hill. It was established around 1880 and closed in 1916. Although a fairly large glasshouse it produced vases little better than 'crib' ware. The vases were any size up to 30 cm (12 in) high, in many colours, but green predominated. Their speciality was epergnes, from singles to six-way, but their long low epergnes 3 mm ($\frac{1}{8}$ in) diameter, wire-twisted into rings from 20–45 cm (8–18 in) long, carrying up to nine trumpets, were turned out by the thousand. Other firms made them, but generally of a much better quality. For what it is worth, the firm often claimed that it exported more coloured glass than any other glassworks in England. A few years before the First World War, George Carder, Frederick's brother, was appointed Manager. Like many others he tried to produce 'Burmese' but actually achieved 'Flambeau'. They were one of the few firms to make all of their

coloured ware pay. George Carder changed back to crystal, I don't know whether it was this change in policy or because of World War I, but the firm closed down soon after.

J. F. Bolton Bowater, Platts Glass Works, Amblecote, worked in crystal and colour. They made the usual crystal tableware – epergnes, sugar and creams, and vases etc., in colour, but also bought from other glassworks. T. Evans who owned a crib, would bring in glass from Bromsgrove, see **168**.

Many other glassworks abounded in the immediate Stourbridge area, but as their types of glassware were similar to some of that described, I will pass on to the Dudley firms.

Research here has proved very disappointing, for numerous works called themselves glasshouses, but only Thomas Hawkes, Dudley Glass Works, Stone Street, would seem to have made any that is really worthy of collecting. Established in 1766, it closed in 1842, Benjamin Richardson was the Works Manager. Unfortunately very few authentic pieces exist but I believe the Dudley Museum has one or two pieces of crystal, coloured specimens are very few, see **287**.

The Birmingham region

This region was a much more compact one than its neighbour, Stourbridge, but there was a larger number of glassworks. These produced coloured glass in large quantities, but the production was in no way equal to that of the Stourbridge area. This was probably because the emphasis was on crystal, and I must repeat, that the production of crystal ware was the life-blood of the industry. With the population rising, factory owners were 'output conscious' because the man in the street wanted more and cheaper glass.

Some of the Birmingham factories made types very similar to those of Stourbridge, but there were differences, and the collector must learn to distinguish one from another. In particular he must be able to recognize quality, for much of Birmingham's coloured ware production was of a commercial quality.

The firm of G. Bacchus is important for any collector because they were more art conscious. It was established in 1818 as Bacchus, Green and Green, Union Glassworks, Dartmouth Street and it changed hands many times until in 1860 the Bacchus family sold out to Stone, Fawdry and Stone. In 1841 it was trading simply as George Bacchus and Sons, and it was about that time that it produced both smooth and fancy ware. The output was varied and the quality good. In fact, type for type it was the equal of any Stourbridge glass. Their stand at the Great Exhibition of 1851 proved that they were capable of making anything that their competitors could produce.

When Sir Ben Stone entered the Company in 1860 a brilliant brain was added to an already well-established Company. Stone was a great friend of the Richardson family of Wordsley and this may account for the fact that many of the Bacchus' designs were similar to those of Richardson's. Letters, Accounts, etc., of the late Sir Ben Stone relating to the Union Glass Works 1817–82, can be seen in the Birmingham Reference Library, Catalogue No. 370962 zz 35.

The firm of Lloyd and Summerfield, Park Glass Works, Spring Hill, produced some of the most unusual shapes in both crystal and coloured glass that has ever been made in England. Although it is not my intention to write about crystal, I feel that I should point out that this firm specialized in designs totally foreign to the accepted functional shapes prevailing at that time. The Art Journal of 1850 stated that they made coloured vases shaped like the onion family (see **137 & 138**). Their coloured ware, both smooth and fancy was subject to some extravaganza, but not so extreme as their crystal.

Glass made by Rice, Harris and Sons, Islington Glass Works (1818–60), has always eluded me, but it is important to have some idea of the styles and types which they produced. I can only recommend the reader to the Illustrated Catalogue of the Great Exhibition 1851, pages 182–3. These can be seen in the Reference Section of any good Public Library. J. R. Harris of Belmont Row Glass Works, Great Brook Street, is believed to be the same firm.

Facts concerning F. & C. Osler, Broad Street, (1807–1960) are very difficult to find, in particular facts concerning their fancy ware. I still intend to talk with some of their former employees who are alive, though scattered around the country. Oslers were the people who made crystal drops and pendants, but knowledge concerning their other products is limited. Their table services, both crystal and self-coloured, especially ruby, had no equal. Machine-pressed, opaque busts of well-known people of the Victorian era were also their speciality, and like so many Birmingham glassworks, they also made paperweights.

Mr. Edgar N. Hiley in his book *Brass Saga* gives a very detailed account of Thomas Osler's entry into the glass trade. He says that Mr. Osler and Mr. Shakespeare who had a glasshouse at Hockley making 'Glass Toys',

opened up in business in Great Charles Street in 1807. Some time later they made samples of 'Icicle Drops' for a stranger and this possibly led to their manufacture of drops and pendants and eventually to candelabra and chandeliers.

Oslers were well-known in the Midlands. They exhibited at the Birmingham Exhibition in Broad Street in 1849. Their crowning glory was when Queen Victoria ordered from them a pair of candelabra, 2.4 m (8 ft) in height, each with fifteen lights. Their famous glass fountain was the centre of attraction at the 1851 Exhibition. Four tons of colourless crystal, it was 8.2 m (27 ft) in height, easily converted to a superb candelabrum.

Research into the Victorian period proves the popularity of chandeliers, table lamps, lustres and other shelf ornaments, some made with only three droppers. Almost half of the Birmingham manufacturers were solely dependent on this type of article. In the 1840s most of the firms were making their own pendants and droppers, but Oslers established what must have been the first conveyor belt system in the glass trade. It consisted of a long table and along one side of which were seated some twenty girls. The pendants when first formed were very rough and they were smoothed by the girls, the first one using a rough emery powder, the second a less rough powder and so on to a very fine powder until the pendant was polished. The final operation was the drilling of the small holes. This new system eventually gave Oslers a monopoly in the pendant and drop trade.

Messrs. Blew & Son were brass casters and if you examine **139** it is obvious why I must mention this firm. As can be seen from the illustration, two brass castings are fastened around the vase. Hooks grip the top of the vase, and screws fasten the two castings on to a foot ring. The ageing of the brass castings adds much to the attraction of this piece. Although both gold and silver are common forms of decoration on glass, brass or bronze in this form is most unusual.

Birmingham appears to be the only centre for this type of work in the 1850s when a number of glasshouses bought castings to add interest to their products. G. Bacchus and F. & C. Osler were good customers for these and other types of castings, and they displayed glass decorated in this way at the 1851 Exhibition. Blew & Son also purchased from Richardson's of Wordsley, coloured shades and cased stems for special candle lamps which they made and sold.

Messrs. John Walsh, Walsh, Soho and Vesta Glass Works, Lodge Road, Birmingham (1854–1952) produced a great deal of crystal but their coloured ware was a very important part of their output. Their combined crystal and coloured glass is very attractive to the eye, colour is a vast range with no one colour predominating. They made both smooth and fancy ware according to the whims of the public. Their output was huge. In the firm's long history they must have made the majority of the styles and types produced by other firms in the Midlands. But they commercialized the styles, they cheapened them. Even their 'one-off' specimens give the appearance of being mass produced. Some few years before the firm closed they became interested in cheap machine-pressed glass – possibly a cause of their decline?

Paperweights were also a common feature of Birmingham's production. These were made in large quantities but were generally poor in quality and mostly of the millefiore type.

Three firms in Birmingham traded under the name of Barnes. Isaac Barnes, Cambridge Street, Broad Street, Summer Row, 1855–75; Francis Barnes (Coloured glass) Barr Street, Great Hampton Row, until 1858; G. H. Barnes, Warstone Lane, Hockley, until 1890. Other notable firms in the region were: W. Gammon & Son, Great Brook Street, 1829–87; Hands Glassworks, Lodge Road, crystal and coloured glass, closed down in 1930; J. R. Harris, Belmont Row Glass Works, Great Brook Street, until 1812, believed to be R. Harris of Islington Row; Parker & Sanders, Toledo Works, Aston, Aston Brook Street.

The London region

Searching for the coloured Victorian glass of this region has always been most disappointing, for me. Glass was made, but most of it was cut or engraved. The glass produced in the Regency period although 'stiff', was very elegant, thought in its design and skill in its manufacture were certainly not lacking, and the brilliancy was generally achieved by cleverly positioned deep-cutting. A change in decoration came in the 1820s when less cutting and much more engraving was used, especially for the better class tableware which was produced in thinner metal.

Although exquisitely engraved wines had been made in Britain in the previous century, copper-wheel engraving was particularly popular in London for some forty years in the first half of the Victorian period.

Certain artists from Germany settled in the London area and glass firms there were eager to use their skill. It was probably this emphasis on engraving which accounted for the late introduction of colour by London glass manufacturers and the slow development of the smooth period.

During the first half of the nineteenth century, opal jugs and vases, some plain, some enamelled, were produced by London firms, but only in small numbers. These were well-designed and undoubtedly owe their elegance to French influence. Most of the pieces that remain today, generally signed, are in museums, or hold pride of place as family heirlooms. A collector will be very fortunate if he can obtain one of these early smooth period specimens. A period of smooth ware was developing, and this continued until the Great Exhibition of 1851, which gave an enormous impetus to cased glass manufacture.

There had been some experimentation in Britain with this type of product prior to 1851, but at the Exhibition, the German glass firms showed the world the 'ultimate' in cased glass. It also showed our own very limited knowledge of casing glass.

Another style displayed in 1851 was silvered glass patented by Varnish & Co. of London. This was cased glass with a difference, for the two casings were made with a layer of air between them and this air space was filled with mercury which then adhered to the inner surfaces before the casings were sealed. This glass could be both cut and engraved, and was made in a number of colours. There were problems in its manufacture and, as a consequence, was only produced for a short period, 1849–52. It was, however, copied in both Germany and the United States.

The Bermondsey Glass Company which closed in 1914 produced some interesting pieces of 'Applied Art'. The firm made both pressed and free-blown glass.

Gray-Stan Glass (1926–36) was a small company situated in the very heart of London which has been fully researched by Albert Revi. This firm produced some very fine art glass, all made entirely by hand, and very few pieces were the same.

But, in my opinion, the elite of London glass over the whole period, and until very recently, has been produced by Whitefriars. Sadly, they have ceased trading and their works are to be demolished, but Caithness Glass in Scotland hope to continue the name. Powell took colour to Whitefriars from Bristol in the early eighteenth century and their cased glass and paperweights are well-known, as is their speciality of millefiore paperweights. As with other glassworks, crystal was the backbone of their production, but sometimes added to this crystal were very subdued self-colours in the form of applied prunts, tear-drops and threads in patterns.

The Northern region

This region is not only a very large one in area, but it also includes a phenomenal number of glassworks. To name only a tenth of these and attribute to each its own styles and types is too much to ask in a book of this size, even if I had the knowledge to do it. A little research shows that at least fifty per cent of the output of both large and small firms was machine-pressed in the period 1850–1930, the remainder being free-blown crystal. But much of the machine-pressed ware that was produced should not, in my opinion, concern a collector. I shall, therefore, concentrate on those firms which I feel produced specimens worth buying.

Molineaux Webb, Manchester Flint Glass Works, Kirby Street, Cannel Street, Ancoats, Manchester, produced very interesting glass during the period 1827–1929. The Mr. Webb was no relation to the Webbs of the Stourbridge area. By the year 1850 the output of this firm exceeded twenty-five tons a week, but their catalogues always emphasized crystal tableware, and made little mention of colour. The same or very similar articles were produced by both free-blown and machine-pressed methods and there was very little difference in the final product when we consider that the cutting wheel cannot compete with the machine in the flexibility of pattern produced.

Their opal vases decorated with classical figures, especially those in monochrome should not be mis-taken for Richardson's of Stourbridge. Both firms, it seems, took many of their ideas from 'Vases from the Collection of Sir Henry Englefield Bt.' published in 1819, and illustrated by H. Moses. Although many specimens were registered, I have never been able to discover a trademark for this firm. I have no infor-mation concerning the firms of Thomas Molineaux, 2 Beswick Street, Manchester (1828) and Maginnis Molle & Co. of Kirby Street, Ancoats, Manchester (1829), but I feel that these were part of the firm of Molineaux Webb eventually.

Of the other first-class glass manufacturing firms, I next choose H. Greener, Wear Flint Glass Works, Sunderland, established shortly before 1827, (now James A. Jobling & Co. Ltd.), because they were most

adventurous in design. Crystal tableware and also ornaments figured prominently in their output, but little is known of their cutting and engraved products. Many of their pressed articles were also made plain and some were engraved. An example of their engraving is found on many of the rummers depicting the Sunderland Bridge. Greener's pressed glass is generally of a brighter crystal than most, and in a variety of colours, some opalescent, many pieces have acid-etched patterns, while a few were wheel-engraved. The wine glass of H. Greener, 344, seems a little out of place. Even the most observant collector might pass it by. Please note its characteristics as stated in the caption.

Sowerby's Ellison Glass Works of East Street, Gateshead, was established in the 1760s. The Sowerby family had four glassworks in Britain and also one in Belgium. I only learnt of this recently when I purchased one of their vases which had their trademark enclosed with the words 'British Made'. They were one of the first firms to produce pressed glass and developed a form of moulded glass called 'Vitro-porcelain' which was opaque and commonly called slag glass. Slag was made in four plain colours – black, white, yellow and turquoise-blue, as well as in a variety of mixtures of those colours.

George Davidson & Co. Ltd., Teams Glass Works, Gateshead, was not established until 1867. I was astounded at the number of patents granted to Thomas Davidson (1860–1937) but people from the firm told me that he could do almost anything with pressed glass! There is a close similarity in the design of their ornaments and those of Sowerby's, but this will be discussed later. Davidson's and Sowerby's turned out every conceivable product made from glass – hats, walking sticks, pistols, twin bottles, bellows, pipes and all sorts of tableware, and Davidson's, I understand, also made some paperweights.

We must also consider the glass made by Messrs. Edward Moore, Tyne Flint Glass Works, West Holborn, South Shields, who, in 1851, took over premises previously occupied by Messrs. Cook & Son. The firm, which closed in 1913, classed themselves as pressed glass manufacturers from the outset. Recently a ref-erence has been discovered to Edward Moore purchas-ing a mould from Joseph Webb of Stourbridge (1887). This raises a number of questions, for Stourbridge has never been considered as a pressed glass centre.

Warrington in Lancashire was also a very important glass centre in Victorian times. The lack of knowledge about its glassworks can, I think, be accounted for by the fact that it was not a chartered town until 1847. Only recently was I able to discover the trademark (and then only the one for pressed glass) of the most important firm there, Robinson & Co. Ltd., Warrington Bank Quay Works, also called the Mersey Flint Glass Works. Like Sowerby's, a number of members of the family established small works, finally amalgamating in 1869. The firm was originally established as Glazebrook & Robinson, Oxford Lane, in 1797. It closed in 1933 and transferred to Birmingham, adjoining the premises of J. Walsh, Walsh Ltd., but trading under its own name. The usual crystal tableware formed a good percentage of this firm's output, but coloured ornamental articles and pressed crystal were also made in large quantities. Their 'Empress' glass, some of the earliest pressed crystal, was a great success.

But it was the glassworks of Manchester and the immediate surrounding area where I believe more styles and types of glassware were made than in any other centre in England. In addition to Molineaux Webb, already mentioned, there were other individual glassworks, making similar articles but not under one roof. However, Burtles, Tate & Co. of Poland Street, Oldham Road, established in 1858 and closing in 1924, were not exaggerating in their catalogues which stated that they made flint and coloured, pressed and blown, ornamental, fancy and novelties.

J. Derbyshire & Co., established in 1856, was a firm which produced first-class articles and should be noted, in particular for their Landseer Lions. This company's products deserve careful consideration.

Like Birmingham and Stourbridge, the Manchester area was also a centre for epergnes. But unlike the type produced in the Midland centres, the Manchester ones were strong, heavy and useful. In fact, if there is a common denominator for the great variety of glass produced in this region it is, in my opinion, its apparent 'strength'. There is generally a minimum of decoration, and the glass looks sturdy and is mostly utilitarian.

I stated earlier that although no glass was made in the Bristol area during this period, (and by this I mean no glass of interest to me and my collection) the styles made there in the eighteenth century influenced the glass in other areas later and in particular Lancashire.

The Nailsea style started with the early splashed glass from Bristol around the middle of the eighteenth century. By chance, some of the splashes would form crescents when the glass was blown, and the development of this to organized patterned crescents is obvious. It was this idea that influenced the development of glass in the Manchester district where the Nailsea style generally was worked into a crystal background.

The reader may have examples of the style which he knows were made in the Stourbridge area and I would suggest that he takes a close look at those specimens. He will observe that the crescents in pattern form, made in the Stourbridge area between 1880 and 1940, were applied in a totally different way from those produced either in the Bristol or Manchester areas. They were applied threads worked on to the body of the glass, and nearly always on to opaque colours. But more of this development in the next chapter, British glass in detail.

The Scottish region

The Scottish region is not a fruitful one for collectors of Victorian coloured glass. As far as I can ascertain there seem to be two periods only, 1870–1900 and 1924–50.

The first period includes 'Clutha' made by James Couper & Sons, City Glass Co., Glasgow. James Couper's introduction to the glass trade was in 1832 with A. & R. Cockran but he built his own glassworks in 1850. Very little glass worth collecting was made after 1900, and the firm was closed in 1921, see **238**, **239** and **240**.

About forty kilometres (twenty-five miles) to the north of Glasgow is Alloa. My research into Alloa glass is very limited. The whole district seemed to be centred around bottle manufacturing and their unique types of decoration. The Nailsea-type specimens attributed to Alloa are fascinating but lack that skilled control and finish of the Manchester area.

Perth, another forty kilometres (twenty-five miles) north, was the centre of the revival of decorative smooth style 'Monart', made by John Moncrieff Ltd., North British Glassworks and established in 1865. 'Monart' is a name, representing Moncrieff and Ysart. Salvador Ysart and four of his sons, started the development of Monart in 1924. It was continued until World War II began in 1939. In 1950 production was resumed but since so many skilled men had left, it was decided to cease manufacture. Salvador and two of his sons had started a small glassworks on 'The Shore' by the River Tay, trading as Vasart Glass Ltd. By 1964 when the old Vasart works had been demolished it was under new management and re-opened as Strathearn Glass at Crieff. I am aware that we have passed the Victorian period, but many collectors have asked me about Vasart, for more details see **237**.

British glass in detail

One very important point to remember, although many readers will already be aware of it, is that the registered date of any article is generally the year when production of that article began. Production might have been maintained for months or weeks only, but it could have continued for years. The registered date therefore does not always denote an exact age. We will proceed chronologically as much as possible, but some overlapping will obviously occur.

Throughout the Victorian period, as stated earlier, glassware styles were divided into 'Smooth' and 'Fancy', so articles without any appendages, other than handles, were 'Smooth' and the vitrified examples, **6–10**, come under that category.

Richardson Vitrified Enamel Color (and that was their way of spelling the word 'colour') was registered in 1847. Many collectors have their own reasons as to why the 'U' should be missing, but there is no official explanation. I am not sure why the word 'color' occurs in the registration at all and whether it refers to the coloured decoration or to the glass mixture, but I do know that, with the exception of opal, all coloured mixtures are dated later. The original opal, by the way, is rather poor, for in many cases the particles of potash have not dissolved. See also **127** and **130**.

Following on from vitrified came alabaster, another mixture of opal, see **11–15**. Richardson's didn't always sign their alabaster pieces on the base, so if the article has handles try looking under the base of a handle for a signature. Most of the specimens are thick and heavy compared with vitrified, the latter being very sedate, rarely going beyond classical shapes, with decoration just as 'serious' but alabaster goods were unlimited, and many pieces look magnificent, although today they are a very poor second for price.

On reflection, I think even to try to compare alabaster from different glassworks is almost impossible. Discussing the problem with an authority on glass mixtures I came to the conclusion that the glassblowers had solved the issue by calling it 'opal', whoever made it. As collectors must have some guidance, there is one definite fact, alabaster can be one of two kinds, opaque or translucent. Other than that, Richardson's and Stevens & Williams's alabaster is similar in name only.

Richardson's alabaster is opaque, whereas Stevens & Williams's can be opaque or translucent. Translucency can be obtained by building up a thickness in layers of the same mixture; Stevens & Williams improved on this by applying a coloured casing (little more than a stain) to which they gave names such as Rose-du-Barry, jade and blue, etc. (see **84–90**). Only occasionally is a self-coloured translucent alabaster specimen found. Alabaster made at other English glasshouses never seemed to acquire the popularity of that produced by these two Stourbridge firms.

However, Frederick Carder, after living in America for a number of years, used it for many of his special and commercial types, not that he altered the glass mixture much, but used it as a base for new or improved styles of decoration.

The examples of iridescent crystal over opal are commercial, but some very nice art pieces were made, and are worth seeking out, see **16–20**.

Years before the Great Exhibition of 1851, British glass manufacturers knew that their German rivals were producing cased glass (overlay), but they did not realize just how superior their skill was until they saw the Continental products displayed. The foreign manufacturers, however, did make one mistake – they tended to remain commercial. The British had little chance of excelling them, although a number of firms did make an effort, but it was left to Ben Richardson, that fine Stourbridge glassmaker, and G. Bacchus & Sons of Birmingham who were joined by Benjamin Stone (later to be Sir Benjamin Stone) to equal and, in some cases, overtake them, chiefly in design. Within a few years both firms were producing saleable cased glass for cutting and engraving, but each developed its own style in shapes and pattern design, see **21–35**.

Many of the specimens made by G. Bacchus & Sons are unique in form and really defy description, so I suggest that the collector, whenever possible, should read art journals dated from 1850, in which drawings of their glassware can be found. Richardson's kept to simple and well-tried shapes but with the occasional lapse in design. They often copied certain cased Bohemian vases and the result is that so many of their specimens are so alike that it is almost impossible to separate one from another. In many cases, however, this can be done. First turn the vase over and examine the base. The German specimen is always ground perfectly flat, taking out the pontil (that is if it ever had one). Richardson's also ground the base, but did not trouble to remove the pontil completely, or even the overlapping casing colours.

A further check can be made by using the ultraviolet lamp. Place a signed piece of Richardson's alabaster and any cased opal vase side by side, and note the colours. If the opals are identical, additional proof is hardly necessary.

This is perhaps the place to clear up any mis-understanding some may have concerning cased and overlay glass. Theoretically there is no difference, but the description 'overlay' is now generally used in connection with cutting, when the thickness (up to a point) of the outer case does not matter. When the article is required for cameo, thickness and colour have to be considered, because colours vary with hardness, and this in turn has to be considered with design.

The cane filigree used in the decoration of jugs and vases are exactly the same as used in paperweights, but in longer lengths, see **42**, **43** and **46**. In paperweights the canes are in short lengths and placed as a pattern, then enclosed. When used in vases, etc., the canes, as well as being stretched are also marvered, or pressed, into the glass, which turn them into coloured stripes or bands. This type of decoration is started in a mould, but it is only skill which will produce a perfectly formed pattern.

Venetian glassworkers made magnificent specimens of this type of glassware, but in my opinion the firm of St. Louis, France, has no equal. I suggest that the reader should examine a few cane-decorated vases by St. Louis

before forming an opinion of any other specimens of this type of glassware.

I am not sure that the decoration the Japanese called 'Matsu-No-Ke' was registered, but it was commonly used when referring to Stevens & Williams's applied decoration, see **59** and **60**.

The rocketing price of 'Burmese' glass recently has encouraged many glassworks to produce similar articles, and during the last ten years a few firms in the United States and Italy have marketed modern examples. When looking at the specimens **65–78**, the reader should note the colour and pattern only. Not a great deal of information I admit, but let me add immediately that few experienced collectors are deceived after, and only after, comparing the old with the new.

Most readers are familiar with the origin of this type of glass but for those who are not, here are the essential facts. Frederick Shirley, an American, patented the Burmese mixture in 1885. I am not sure of Mr. Shirley's standing with The Mount Washington Glass Co., New Bedford, Massachusetts, USA, but in 1886 that company applied for, and was granted, the right to manufacture articles in Burmese. The trademark in the form of an ellipse was registered No. 56,859 16 December, 1885. The reader will notice one year's difference, but I checked the dates and the register shows 1886 as the application date, while the trademark is 1885. In 1886 Thomas Webb purchased the rights to manufacture Burmese in England, and their application was registered on 11 September, 1886, a week *before* that of The Mount Washington Glass Co.

Registered No. 56,664, the trademark has the words 'Queen's Burmese Thomas Webb & Sons, Patent' on an impressed disc. What is not generally known is that, after a time, Thomas Webb altered the mixture slightly, making the colour much richer, examples **68** and **69** nicely demonstrate this point. Although Thomas Webb had purchased the rights to manufacture Burmese the formula was common knowledge in Stourbridge and, in fact, some lovely pieces were made at other factories just to prove they could make it, but these were never offered for sale.

Turning to modern types, colour is a very good guide, but many of the pieces are mould blown and also carry a pontil mark. Since these 'modern' pieces have been on sale the general public has adopted a very sensible attitude. People only pay good money for signed pieces.

If one cares to study Thomas Webb's enamel decoration, this is almost as good as a trademark, but be careful, for this, too, has been copied. There is another test, rather difficult to decide sometimes, but it might help; colours look opaque, but when the mixture was first patented it was translucent, so holding the article up to a bright light does help.

A few words about 'Silveria', a type of glassware by which particles of mica-fleck or pieces of silver foil, are trapped between two layers of glass, made by Stevens & Williams c. 1900, see **93–5**. This may be of great importance to some collectors, because of its value. The price of this glass has risen tremendously over the past five years. The idea of sandwiching very thin metal foil between glass layers was not new or for that matter successful, but Silveria in its final form did have a certain attraction for some people. I think it was the 'unreal' quality of each specimen that sold it. There are lots of pieces of this type with various sizes of fleck, but those specimens with foil are not so plentiful.

The paperweight is included to show readers the colours and style used in the making of true Silveria. In the actual vases, foil is added, and surfaces are ruffled, but they are not necessarily rough. In many cases the surface is irregularly grooved and the neck twisted.

In this chapter I am particularly interested in glassware which is controversial. This is intentional, for in this way collectors can read an opinion which is not necessarily the accepted one. Take splashed glass as an example, see **96–7**. Whenever I see a gaudy splashed piece, I make the first mental note, 'foreign'. If the vase has a ground flat top, a hollow foot, no pontil mark, and thin sides, I have to be persuaded, against all instinct, that it *is* English. This is not to say that English glassworkers never used these methods, but on the rare occasions they did, it would be a deliberate act and not their usual practice. Splashed glass was, of course, made throughout Britain, but the dabs of colour were subdued or in pastel shades which could also be seen to form a design.

I have examined **121** very carefully and I cannot offer a definite explanation. The cane pattern was the one used on a series of small jugs, but the foot formation was used by Thomas Webb. The answer would seem to be that one of Thomas Webb's former glass-blowers was working at Stevens & Williams during the manufacture of this dish.

In the illustration **152** we see a vase which could have been one of a series depicting British naval engagements, if fate had not intervened. In 1930 John Jenkins, Glass Merchant, Holborn Viaduct, London, had an idea to issue a number of pressed vases similar to the one shown, but each different. To be sure of accuracy of detail, he copied from engravings exhibited at the National Maritime Gallery, Greenwich, London. A few moulds were made and submitted to various English glassworks which, for a variety of reasons, were unable or unwilling to co-operate. He tried and was successful with a Czechoslovakian firm, but in 1935 was advised to withdraw his moulds, because of pending hostilities.

What I failed to do, was to ask Mr. Jenkins what kind of specimens had been made and how many. He did tell me, however, that only a few of the naval examples had been supplied. Later I found many with a floral design, and obviously these had been the first issued. Regarding signatures, the specimen shown is signed with the trademark 'Barolac' in block letters on the base. Most of the floral specimens have 'Made in Czecho-Slovakia' but not all have the trademark.

Further comment is necessary on **192**. The illustration clearly shows the formation of the six sides. This effect is obtained by the tools used, and there is no reason why any number of sides cannot be obtained. As the shape is so uncommon, the reader will easily visualize it either as a bowl or lampshade, with or without a base. When one is discovered, Thomas Webb must be considered as the makers.

Opalescent glassware has been the Cinderella of the glass trade for far too long, but there are two kinds from which the collector has to choose. The easily-made pieces are generally 'rubbish' and a waste of time to collect. Those produced by a designer and a first-class glass-blower deserve attention. I have always admired this glass and at every opportunity have purchased it, see **199–228**. My advice for the collector without experience, is always to examine and study any piece of interest, because with this type of glassware it is not always what you like, but how difficult the piece was to make.

I have previously used the word experience and, in this case, it means recognizing the glass-blower's skill, and, I am sorry to say, this just cannot be explained. There may be, however, one piece of useful advice. An extravagantly shaped piece with the opalescence in awkward places, is always good. Coloured deserves extra attention: blue opalescent is the most difficult to produce and find.

For the benefit of younger readers I will explain what the examples 204–7 were used for during the Victorian period. In many homes Sunday-tea was laid out in what was called 'The Front Room'. After tea the table was cleared and covered with a fancy table-cloth, on which were placed these ornaments in the following order. The largest was placed in the centre of the table, the other three in order of height as shown in the illustration. Most of the time there were three equally spaced rows radiating from the centre decoration. Occasionally there were four lines of ornaments. The specimen with opalescent trumpets (208) is one of another pattern used for the same purpose.

Anything that occurs frequently in glass specimens must always be memorized, be it style, shape or colour, something unusual that attracts, perhaps a foot and stem, but more often the top, for this can generally decide its provenance. Illustrations 211 and 224 have a top formation which, although uncommon, took me years to track down to their manufacturer. You say it could be copied? It was, but the finish of the shape is special, Richardson's always heated the edges, a means of removing all sharp points.

Colour, also, is a guide with both specimens. 211 would have looked better with more uranium in the mixture, although Richardson's never used this element to excess. In 224, green, a favourite colour with Richardson's is used to stop opalescent development and form a straight line. Two 'minor' specimens, but both full of character.

I have collected 'Clutha' for years, but it has never been a favourite of mine. However, this kind of attitude must never influence collecting, because all types are essential to show development. References to a disagreement between James Couper & Son and Thomas Webb regarding 'Clutha', I have seen many times, but at the moment I cannot find any evidence that a similar glassware to 'Clutha' was made by the Stourbridge firm. One thing is certain. It was not a definite glass mixture, otherwise it would have been recorded, for this was, and still is, a glasswork's ritual. This is not an exercise to settle an argument, but to find out if there is any sense in trying to find a specimen which may not exist!

I would like to elaborate on what I call Webb's soda-lime series, see 243–4, 246–7 and 284. The specimens have a lead content, but do not ring when struck. It has become a habit with most people interested in glass to flick the article with a fingernail, and if the glass is lead crystal it should emit a clear ringing sound. The articles I refer to as the soda-lime series have a lead mixture, but coupled with design and thickness the ringing sound is replaced by a dull thud. Knowing that all collectors and glassworkers use this method my expression of soda-lime tells them just what to expect.

Collectors will find with experience that most glass-works had favourite colours, but sometimes costs limited their use. Likewise collectors will find that certain colours register very quickly. Try to cultivate a memory for colours for it is a very important part of collecting. I have noticed how easily old glassmen can recognize where a piece of glass was made by its colours.

Richardson's yellow and green are outstanding and, although they made about six shades of green, all are bright. The green vitrified has white flecks, see 8 and 9, and these have to be looked for. Note the depth of colour in 49 and 254. 256 is the same yellow as 254, but used as a casing over opal which tends to reduce its colour density.

'Flakestone' ware, see 255, is not splashed (sploshed) glass. As already stated splashed glass was not popular glassware in the Stourbridge area, but Flakestone was made at Richardson's and Thomas Webb's and both firms followed the same production methods. At times they may have accidentally arrived at the same shape, but in colour terms the difference is very distinct. In simple terms, small pieces of sheet glass, in any colour, thickness or shape are marvered (pressed) between two casings, the inner one can be of any colour, but the outer case is always crystal.

There is nothing haphazard in the making. From its design stage, the background colour, size, thickness and colour of the small pieces encased, all have their allotted place. When finished, these pieces are fairly heavy.

Hocks, (see 260 for an English example) must originate from Germany. It is sad that they have not been collected more eagerly, for their decoration covers the entire range of methods used in the glass industry. Perhaps it is not too late now, although prices could prohibit all but the most enthusiastic and rich.

An offspring from hocks are Edwardian wines, very

similar in proportion, but shorter, and the bowl is more conventional. I have noticed that these are still plentiful.

Richardson's evidently tried to cash in on the success of Stevens & Williams's 'Jewel' glassware. Their articles were just as well made, perhaps better, but their specimens lacked grace and consistency, their articles included all the techniques used in their competitor's glassware, but they were not 'organized' in design. Compare the two specimens **262** and **263** with any of the Jewel series, see **52** and **79–81**, and perhaps you will see what I mean.

After 1945 Stevens & Williams had problems similar to most other glass firms, one particular problem being the fast production of saleable goods. With coloured glass which they had in stock, they designed and produced types such as 'Abbey' and 'Regal' glassware.

267 and **268** are examples of Abbey which could easily be attributed to the mid-nineteenth century. The first impression is that the crushed particles of coloured glass are part of the batch (mixture) but they were obviously marvered into the crystal during the blowing stage.

An example of 'Regal', **293**, has red, blue and green spiral bands running parallel. These are found in crystal vases, some of which have ground circular areas forming a pattern. Examine the illustration carefully as other shapes were made. Please note the date, 1945.

I do not think that collectors can in any way be misled when they find a coloured glass tulip. Richardson's, I believe, was the only English firm to specialize in their making. The one illustrated is one of a number of series, and is the common type. Some of them are elegant and only the finest craftsmen could have produced them.

One type had a fault, a stem that was too thin and which was easily broken. The flower heads were sold to lamp-workers who welded on their own idea of 'feet'. Any of these in colour are worth collecting, but not the modern crystal ones.

Crocodiles, hand-pressed like the one shown, are now being circulated in the Midlands in many colours, but as far as I am aware, not in lemon opalescent, as were the old ones.

The example of 'Mirror Glass', **275**, made by the Edinburgh Crystal Glass Co., is plain, but most are decorated by cutting. Please do not be misled into thinking that this is the same as the glassware made by Varnish & Co., London 1849, see **318–321**. It is similar in looks only; the London glassware is one of the most rare and expensive types of glass ever made in Britain.

The glassmakers' habit of imitating other materials during periods of trade depression can prove very interesting for collectors. Tableware utensils were copied but ornaments made of unusual materials were not neglected. We have already seen glass imitating wax and **278** is imitating stone.

The caption to **283** refers to a similarity of colour between H. Northwood's Carnival and Stevens & Williams's iridescent. I am only suggesting that they both used similar oxides to obtain their colours, the articles themselves are totally different. Whereas H. Northwood's carnival was pressed, Stevens & Williams's specimens were free-blown in many forms, salt cellars with various top formations are fairly common, but all are iridescent *only* at the top.

I have spoken about Thomas Hawkes, Dudley Glass-works, before. It is assumed, and I think so too, that they produced first-class glassware in colour and crystal equal to any made anywhere in England, see **287**. The names of the owners, where the glassworks stood, and when it was demolished, are common knowledge in the glass fraternity, yet other than a few specimens of glass handed down through families there is no evidence regarding their styles and types of glassware. Research is really needed here.

The assumption that Richardson's never made cheap glassware is ridiculous, see **288**. I worked very close to the factory, and I knew some of the Richardson family and a number of their employees. Some of their glass I purchased when the firm closed down, and I also purchased some of their specimens from Mr. Pargeter's collection, so, did they make any rubbish?

They certainly were capable of making inferior glassware compared with their many first-class pieces. My opinion is that the glass quality varied with the cash available. One thing is certain, the quality of their glassware a few years before the works closed was very commercial.

The formulation of Stevens & Williams's glass mixture 'Dragon's Blood', see **291**, I have always understood was accidental when the firm was developing 'Rockingham'. It sold well, but there is very little to be seen, I believe that the firm itself has only one piece in its Museum. There is a German colour very similar to 'Dragon's Blood' but how close I cannot say, until I get the opportunity to examine the two together. The pieces I have seen are heavy and look typically German, not at all what I would expect from Stevens & Williams.

In my experience machine-pressed cased vases are very difficult to find. **314** and **342** are two excellent examples, each being free-blown before final shaping. **314** is cased opal inside, the top being shaped on the pontil-iron, possibly after pressing. **342** has gone through the whole process of being free-blown and cased before being pressed with combination tools in superb condition. The top is finally ground flat.

Making special pieces to individual requirements is fairly common, but such orders are not generally welcomed. With modern commitments to production this attitude is understandable. But the Victorian period was another world, for glassworkers encouraged anything that increased business.

The practice had not completely died out at Whitefriars as late as 1939. A number of requests they had were 'silly' but occasionally very attractive articles were considered and produced. **326** was one of a number of shapes that fascinated me. Black is a colour which is very difficult to use, but this problem has been surmounted by applying crystal in moderation – a crystal foot in this case.

Most collectors know what the Nailsea pattern is and the emphasis is on the word 'pattern'. The word Nailsea is used so thoughtlessly, even by reputable auctioneers that I think we must have a complete appraisal of what Nailsea means and how we use the word. Nailsea, as a decorative technique, should be understood by all collectors. See **335 & 336**.

Glassworks were started at Nailsea, about thirteen kilometres (eight miles) from the Severn estuary, in c. 1790 by William Chance. Around 1810 a decoration developed which became known as the Nailsea pattern. Robert Lucas Chance, the owner at that time, moved to Spon Lane, Birmingham, and founded Chance Bros. Ltd. At the moment this is all we need to know to investigate the pattern itself. The late Sir Hugh Chance was the leading authority, knowing all the details about his ancestry.

How far the development of the pattern went can be seen in the Bristol Art Gallery and many of the smaller museums in Somerset. I do not think we can include any of this Nailsea glass within the Victorian period because by 1810 Robert Lucas Chance, the man who had begun the development, had left the district. In any case, there seems very little evidence of progress until the pattern moved up-country around 1820, this is my interpretation of the situation from a collector's point of view.

By 1800, or a few years later, we have the original Nailsea glass as little more than bottle glass splashed with white and blue, but there is some doubt about the use of yellow. By the way, if authentic, these specimens are very valuable! About ten years later the Nailsea pattern of crude loops, spirals and swirls had become established and I think this is as far as the Bristol area had gone. The colour had been marvered but was still a surface decoration. We must not forget, however, that although we have agreed that the pattern started in Bristol the Venetians had used loops in a similar manner a hundred years earlier and this was, of course, known to English glassworkers.

The pattern travelled north. In the Midlands, judging by the few pieces found and the lack of interest shown by art journals, the Birmingham glassmen did little more than make the pattern clean and more saleable. What surprises me about the Birmingham attitude is that Robert Lucas Chance, the man who had been so interested in its development in Bristol, should now forsake it, especially as it has been reported that he financially supported some ailing glass firms. His own factory was at Spon Lane, only a short distance from Lloyd and Summerfield, who were not unwilling to try their hand at anything unusual.

The Stourbridge area was more enthusiastic, but it seems they had reservations. It is difficult to pin-point any major reasons and we can only judge by the specimens still in existence. In the first place the pattern never got past the rustic stage, which tells me that although it was made, it was never treated seriously; I cannot find any evidence of it being used commercially. What I have noticed, is that the pattern was used on ceremonial specimens only, and the majority of these are opaque colours. All the opaque coloured pipes, and there are hundreds around from 15 cm (6 in) to 91 cm (36 in) long, are, I feel certain, individual specimens.

The pattern came to fruition around the Manchester area. It is impossible to pick out any individual firm as the particular one which developed the pattern as we know it today, so it is much more sensible to give credit to the area.

Over the years I have tried to follow the development of the Nailsea pattern and two distinct types have emerged. In the Midlands and South, the pattern is generally applied on opaque, rarely on crystal or even transparent colours. In the Northern-region this is reversed, for most of the patterns are on, or in, transparent colours or crystal. I have also seen the pattern made in the form of bubbles. During the mid-1930s one could always be sure of finding a nice example north of Manchester.

I hope collectors will appreciate this information and take careful note of it as it took me a great deal of research over many years to acquire.

I want to draw the reader's attention to the wine signed with H. Greener's trademark, because it has been made in the correct way for an expensive article, see **344**.

So many foreign manufacturers use gilding lavishly that experienced collectors are inclined to overlook the odd treasure. It was because this wine had a blown foot that I examined it so carefully and a few words on how this type of foot was made, could help collectors of early wines as well as those with a particular interest in Victorian glassware.

First, the foot is blown separately as a ball and slightly flattened, then it is joined to the stem which has been drawn out from the bowl on a blowing-iron. The glass is spun to centralize it and the foot is cut off at right angles to the blowing-iron and the whole article passed to a punty. The wine is now finished to shape and size by the person with the punty-iron.

What concerns us with **344** is the foot. During the making, it is usual for a few air bubbles to collect and generally they are eliminated, on the other hand one can easily be missed. It is this one we are looking for and instead of being round, it will be elongated. If a bubble cannot be found, look along the edge of the foot, if it is blown, a small ridge appears on the inside of the foot.

Engraving the trademark must have been an intentional act, although it seems ridiculous as there are so many cheaper ways to mark it.

345 and **349** are two Sowerby's cake dishes with the same pattern and which possibly come from the same mould. The ruby one, **345**, has always been a mystery. The colour I was told by Sowerby's was their latest. I bought one or two pieces of the same colour at the same time some thirty years ago. All are signed with their

trademark, but I have never been able to find a registration date. The other dish, **349**, could possibly be what they advertised as 'Gold' in 1882 although I have always called it 'Carnival'.

When on holiday some twenty-five years ago in the Snowdonia area of Wales, I saw many amber goblets similar to **354**. They were in many cottages and the residents told me they had been sent from America, by their menfolk, who had been laying slate pavements in some parts of New York. Obviously their grandfathers had thought the goblets to be American glass and classified them as 'Gifts from America'. I bought one, thinking it was American glass, it was dated (lozenge) 1872.

After a time, with the design (Rose, Thistle and Shamrock) registered in my mind, I decided to trace it. I found that it had been made by J. Derbyshire of Manchester. It is very easy to guess what had happened!

The specimen **366** has been ground on top, it is one of a pair and I can confirm that the other one has been treated in the same way. Sowerby's, the makers, must have been one of the earliest firms to produce pressed ware. Their early pieces with flat tops c. 1852 have all been ground, that is to say, all those which I have been able to examine. Perhaps there were some early manufacturing difficulties, could this be another pointer for collectors to look out for when identifying Sowerby's early glass?

It is only recently that I have been able to research vases and bowls, signed 'Hailware' made by Hailwood and Ackroyd Ltd., Morley, Leeds. Their shapes are simple, well-balanced and colourful, but unfortunately I have only been able to obtain the example illustrated, see **396**.

All collectors, however wide their experience and knowledge, have difficulties and failures in identification. It is embarrassing when one has identified a piece and along comes some trivial incident which completely alters one's opinion. The following is a situation in which I once found myself.

420 is a blue pressed pipe. When I bought it, I was told that it was a salt cellar, made in the Newcastle-upon-Tyne area, at the turn of the century. This came as no surprise, because I have collected glass salts for years and know that practically every type of English glassware was made into salts, and also that any shape with a fairly deep hollow was sold as a salt.

The Northern region has a reputation for salts in unusual shapes, in fact every region produced its own interpretation of a salt. But 381 is another pipe with 'Souvenir of Ilion N.Y.' painted on the bowl. At first glance it appears to come from the same mould, but measurements show it to be smaller, although this could be explained by the difference in colour contraction. There is no reason to doubt it being a salt, but where was it made, Newcastle or the United States?

432 is a splendid example of Continental applied work, absolutely perfect for pointing out the differences between German and English manufacturing practices.

There is always one feature about Continental glass which we must never forget – most of it was made for export. Foreign designers and glassworks' managements had to remember they were competing, not only in design, but in price, bearing in mind transport costs. As our manufacturers sold most of their goods locally, they could afford to be a little more extravagant with costs. There were, however, other restrictions and a very important one was the fear of breakages! Designers could not ignore this fact and it did hamper their work especially with applied designs and essential handles and jug spouts. This was a most important consideration in design, but colour was possibly their greatest headache, for this was so costly.

Before I continue we must note that there were exceptions, one of which occurred when the German manufacturers tested our markets for their better class specimens and tried to outsell our finer types of glassware. One type was 'Pandora', c. 1900. It was Bohemian (Czechoslovakian after 1918) and to quote the maker's description, 'It is an imitation of ancient Roman glass brought to light by excavations.'

It is a very imaginative type, needing great skill and the correct materials to produce it, all of which made it too expensive for our markets. Nevertheless, it appears from time to time in British antique shops and very occasionally an English reproduction can be found.

The problems foreign glassmakers had then, are now an asset in separating our wares from theirs. When this vase, 432, (one of a pair) was purchased at least twenty years ago, the dealer thought he was offering me beautiful examples of Stourbridge applied work. He was perfectly sincere and was very surprised when I questioned their origin. I will endeavour to make a comparison between this vase and what it would have been like had it been made in England.

First of all, the general shape is much too extravagant for an English piece. There are four different shapes or curvatures placed one above the other. The English designers I feel, would have made the foot and body with one simple curve, gently tapering to a more simple top. The corrugations might be the same, but the folding back of the top would have been less severe, (had it been folded back at all), a top pulled back any more than the one shown is a rarity in English glassware.

Let us also take a look at the foot, hollow and mould blown, together with about 25 mm (1 in) of the body. A thin blown foot of this size is repugnant to English glassblowers, who would have to be ordered to make it so, if it was chosen at all. When a hollow foot is made in England the metal is heavy and the blowers always press down making it almost solid.

The colour is very weak ruby. This is fine unless used in examples like the one illustrated, as large or small diameters look insipid when made from a weak metal. The white top is opal added during manufacture, another sign of a cheap mixture. Had a correctly mixed metal been used, one which would have been more expensive, then re-heating would have achieved the same result. The handles, weak in colour and application, all point to speed to reduce costs.

I have left the flower until last. This was used both on the Continent and in England. In our Northern region it was used more or less in this form throughout the Victorian period but in the Stourbridge region this design finished around 1880. The reason was that John Northwood patented a machine for moulding flowers, which were so much more effective and life-like and so easy to make, that other firms left flowers out of their designs.

Weight, too, must be mentioned, and this is a general rule. Size for size, English specimens are at least fifty percent heavier than their Continental counterparts.

The Bohemian ruby goblet c. 1730, 434, is included so that I can comment on the pattern engraved on the bowl. It is a pattern that may have been used for many years prior to 1730 and I am sure that it did not originate in England. It is chiefly found on crystal specimens, but understanding how it was used adds enormously to a collector's knowledge.

Before we discuss the way it was used in both England and Bohemia there is one item of interest to remember. Whenever this pattern is found on coloured articles and ruby in particular, treat it as Continental until there is positive proof otherwise. In Germany the pattern has always been used in its entirety, but in England engravers sometimes break it down into sections, and at times even add to it, to suit the shape of their article. It is mostly found on expensive glassware, and on specimens which required special skills.

In the early 1930s Thomas Webb produced some 25 cm (10 in) high crystal water jugs. Except for the foot and hollow handle they were completely threaded with crystal, even under the spout. Parts of this pattern were chosen as the main decoration and formed a background for the well-known Stourbridge 'Michaelmas Daisy'. The pattern was enlarged and this allowed it to be cut instead of engraved. It is on this type of expensive glassware that this particular pattern was used. Its use, however, was not confined to any single region in England, and so it is very difficult to specify the district in which a piece was made.

Engraving on coloured glass, which German artists did extensively, helps collectors a great deal with identification, for there was a reluctance on the part of English engravers to follow the German example. Whenever I have asked English glassmen why they disliked engraving on colour, their answer was always that self colours spoil engraving!

Whilst on the subject of patterns here is something which might interest the general reader as well as the collector. This is the engraved 'Willow' pattern. I have never heard of it being used commercially, only on 'specials'. With old engravers it is always spoken of with respect, so to anyone with crystal specimens engraved with this pattern, complete with house, bridge, stream, trees and, of course, the two doves, I say please treat them kindly as they are real treasures.

Cameo must be accepted as one of the most beautiful types of glassware produced during the Victorian period. Hundreds of pictures and thousands of words have praised the designers artists and all those engaged in its manufacture. I knew many of the men and women who toiled to achieve perfection, but for some, the strain was too great. In fact the cost in both time and money forced manufacturers to experiment to find cheaper ways of production.

The breakthrough came with the understanding of the properties of acids, and their ability to dissolve glass. Within a few years cameo became commercial, and I use the word in its worst sense, as some products proved unsaleable. I have limited my comments on this glassware for the reader can find all the information he or she needs in books and magazines devoted exclusively to cameo. It also allows me more space to describe the sort of glass which, although less expensive, is just as desirable from the collector's point of view.

For many years I have wondered when the production of cameo (commercial of course) would recommence. It was obvious as the years passed that, with the use of modern, sophisticated machinery, this would happen and would replace the acid method, and possibly replace engravers. This has now happened.

A few firms in West Germany and England are now producing specimens which are the equal of some of the later Victorian pieces. The technique used to remove superfluous glass is known as sand blasting, a very common practice in other trades, and it is from this, that experiments began and now, one of the leading Stourbridge glasshouses, Webb–Corbett, is happy with its progress and calls its products air-carved, see **436**. I have watched this glassware being developed over the last few years, and with a little more use of pastel shades instead of harsh colours, and more concentration to detail, we can have a product equal to any of the specimens of the Victorian period.

Why have I included a type of modern glassware when we are examining and identifying glass from the earlier period? Because cameo is one hundred per cent Victorian. Many collectors have it, others want it, and so, with fantastic prices involved, the collector must be able to distinguish what is not actually a reproduction, but a type of glassware, which looks like cameo, and is cameo, but is very different when it comes to price.

436 is one of a pair of vases produced by the new method. It was designed by David Smith, who is convinced of its future success, and made by Webb–Corbett.

This specimen, **437**, one of a pair, should be of great interest to all collectors. It looks exactly like an old Birmingham ruby vase c. 1870, a type which, years ago, I would quite often see in Birmingham homes. It was cheap when I bought it and I was happy with my purchase, but I had second thoughts when I examined it carefully at home. In my opinion the shape, size and weight were correct although the top was a little exaggerated. Even the bubbles looked real, but as there was no variation in their size, I was suspicious.

The pair were completely hand-made on the iron, no mould was used to shape the foot and body. They have slight variations in 'minor' areas common in all English types of glassware. The introduction of bubbles is very ingenious, for these are particles of an oxide which expand when mixed with the glass batch (mixture). The foot, although made hollow, has a heavy crystal band worked into the base. The ruby colour is very good, but not gold-ruby, which is what the Birmingham manufacturers would have used. So, after very careful examination, I concluded that they were made in Czechoslovakia.

I contacted a Czechoslovakian firm's representative for his comments. He told me that they were not intended to deceive anyone and that it was the well-balanced style of the vase which had attracted their attention. They were made in four colours including crystal, and, as far as he knew had only been sold by market traders, and not reputable stores.

This is one example of glassware which I have added to my collection to explain an 'original', in this instance a late-nineteenth century Birmingham ruby vase.

Many collectors may be very disappointed with my remarks concerning **438**, a specimen of satin glassware. I have visited many antique shops in Britain where similar pieces have been sold as Stourbridge satin. This was contrary to all my observations and research, as all facts pointed to their being Bohemian. Actually I cannot find one English characteristic. Nevertheless, it is not a bad example of Continental satin.

At times I have considered that some of these were made in Britain to Continental instructions, but even that does not explain some of the points I mention below. Occasionally a piece is found which at first glance seems identical to the one illustrated until it is carefully compared.

First the shape. This is more English than **432**. The ring on the neck which breaks up the distance to the top is not too popular in England, although it was used in a few factories. The exaggerated folds of the top, generally denote Continental, and under no circumstances must a collector when trying to identify a specimen, overlook this formation. This does not mean that English glass-blowers never made any – they did at times, but only for special issues or, curiously, on commemorative pieces. The foot and body up to the ring is mould blown, then transferred to the iron to finish the top. The procedure is routine, but the hollow foot would be flattened to make it solid. In England our glassworkers judge an article by the handle and this is very crude, and the decoration would spoil even a poor specimen.

I have left my comment on colour until last because, in this case, the makers have turned a mediocre piece into a very saleable article by the method of the application of the colour. Initially the jug is made from opal, then a small gathering of red (not ruby) is added to the top and blended on to the outer surface, fading completely before it reaches the base. It appears to be red cased, but this is not strictly true. This was very common practice and very effective.

This is a specimen on which I think all of us would welcome more research. I feel satisfied about the manufacturing details, but was there a possible business deal involved?

In conclusion I would like to add some final comments. For many readers the illustrations and captions may be all that they feel are necessary but I believe some collectors will want to delve much deeper into the subject of identifying glass. I must emphasize that none of my remarks must be used in isolation. I could have made out a list of 'do's' and 'don'ts' but in treating the subject the way I have, I hoped I might encourage my reader's interest and lead him or her on to the path of research.

From experience an ultraviolet lamp is useful, possibly the best way to improve one's knowledge of certain pieces. I have experimented with a lamp for a number of years, it was supplied by P. W. Allen & Co., Liverpool Road, London, Visual Inspection Engineers. Since I cannot find any method to record what I see, I can only make one suggestion that might help collectors.

Every glass firm has its own mixtures for each of its coloured products, the ingredients being recorded in percentages. Under the ultraviolet lamp, glass of the same mixture will reflect the same colour but different mixtures will show up in different colours. One must therefore compare a signed specimen or a piece known to be authentic with an article of uncertain origin. If shades, rather than colours, match exactly there is little reason to doubt that the pieces are from the same firm. This is only a beginning but I feel sure that many will find a way to proceed with confidence, using such a method.

Personalities

On the colour pages you will see hundreds of illustrations of coloured specimens made during the Victorian period. Some, I admit, are not plentiful, and an element of luck will be required to find these. But many are awaiting discovery by the observant and knowledgeable collector.

Who made all this glass? What sort of people were they? Their skill is self-evident. We know they used the ordinary glassmaker's tools, but they also used improvised gadgetry, some of which is found in odd corners of factories even today. But when we sing the praises of well-known personalities, we must not forget their companions who did the rough work, and made success possible.

To me, first-class skills with glass decoration, for truly commercial purposes commenced a few years before 1800. The movement of engravers from Germany and enamellers from France seems to have established London as a decorating centre as opposed to a manufacturing one and this would account for London's late start in colour-work for the Victorian period. But as the craftsmen and women moved north through England they exhibited their skills to local artists who were eager to improve their own work.

By 1860 first-class German engravers had settled in Stourbridge. With the German initiative, certain local engravers tried to emulate their work. Some even improved on it and finally established a reputation. It is men like these, and also those colleagues who backed them up and had to improve their own skills, whom we have to thank for the treasures we collect today. All the prominent individuals had a sound knowledge of all operations in the glass trade, but with all that knowledge they remained specialists at heart, and this is particularly true of the Bohemian engravers. I have been told many times that they rarely mixed socially, that they preferred each other's company, and this is perfectly understandable.

Within a few years of the foreign influx, the local artists had more or less achieved parity of skill. Conditions remained generally good, because skilled decorators were needed for the cameo boom and, of course, for high-class, engraved, overlay specimens. All this activity ceased when World War I commenced. A government order gave all foreign workers the choice of either being interned or going back to their own country. Many returned home and their names and skills have been forgotten. Those who stayed, intermarried, and many are remembered and recorded.

We must remember, however, that the transfer of skills was not a one-way traffic; far from it! A few of the more fortunate of our skilled men visited the Continent looking for new ideas, whilst others (including one of my own relatives) moved to Australia to establish glassmaking there. Some went to America, and these did not disgrace our reputation. The 'overseas movement' started in the Midlands shortly before 1880, but in the north it was much earlier. Among the first emigrants was Joseph Locke. Born in 1846, he was already a brilliant craftsman when he left for America at the age of thirty-seven. His career in England was short but eventful: no young man could have had a better start.

He began his career at Guest Bros. who specialized in all types of glass decoration, then went to Richardson's, Wordsley. Here, with all their knowledge and resources, he rose to be in charge of a number of departments. It was during his time at Richardson's, in about 1878, that he made the second replica of the Portland Vase.

Although his work is not plentiful in England, I have been fortunate to examine some of his cameo and engraving, and in my opinion it is his attention to detail and finish that puts him in the forefront of his companions. American collectors can form their own opinion of the skill of a man, who, when in England, greatly impressed his employer, Ben Richardson, and fellow work-mates. I have often wondered how much the presence of John Northwood in the same village and at the same works, developed the talents of Joseph Locke more than he realized himself.

John Northwood's skill and enterprise placed him amongst the world's greatest glassworkers. Born in 1836, he was trained at Richardson's, as were many others, but the profit from his work had to be his own, so in 1860 with his brother Joseph, he started J. and J. Northwood, Decorators. This brought him into personal contact with glass and china manufacturers, and two people greatly influenced him. One was Sir Benjamin Stone who was Chairman of Stone, Fawdry and Stone, (G. Bacchus & Son) Birmingham and the second, Mr. Joseph Silvers Williams, Chairman of Stevens & Williams.

In 1864 Sir Benjamin Stone had approached John to carve a crystal vase, which he would make at his works in Birmingham, and after some discussion the two men agreed. The 'Elgin' vase was finished in 1873 and it was presented by Sir Benjamin to Birmingham Art Gallery where it is on display. The Elgin vase is 39.5 cm (15½ in) high and Grecian in style, decorated in two very difficult techniques. The decoration around the body is carved and is taken from the Parthenon frieze. The remainder of the decoration is also Grecian but flat, the pattern having been worked by the acid process. It is generally agreed that as the carving is in relief, this vase began the cameo era.

John produced three more hand-worked cameo vases – the Portland Vase replica, the Milton Vase and the Dennis Vase (Pegasus), but his work during the latter part of his life has already been commented upon earlier in the section on Stourbridge as he played such a significant part in the glass industry of the area.

At the peak of the Victorian glass-making era Britain lost two outstanding personalities, Joseph Locke to America and John Northwood who died in 1902.

For hundreds of Midland families glass-making was their whole existence, and the Northwood family was no exception. John's son Harry had gone to America a few years before Joseph Locke, not, I understand with any definite job in sight. He was an excellent glassman, his training I assume was at Richardson's and at his father's place. The family may have some of Harry Northwood's glass, but I have not seen any myself.

Whilst still at school, I had a teacher who was a friend of Harry and Clara Northwood, so before writing this book I made arrangements with her to discuss the holidays she had spent in America with them. She could not tell me anything about his glass, but she had a few pieces he had given her as presents. My impression after our discussions was that Harry Northwood was not very excited when he first examined 'Carnival' glass, which at that time was very popular with the American public. This I can well understand, for he had just arrived from an area where some of the world's finest free-blown art pieces were made, and where, for anyone to mention machine-pressed glass in any form, was to ask for 'trouble'. I know this because of the rude answers I received if ever I spoke about pressed glass to Stourbridge glassmen. I do not think it was the glass itself which they despised, but the possible effect on their jobs. I believe that Harry Northwood thought that if the Americans could make it, so could he, and he did. When he died in 1924, his wife Clara returned to Stourbridge and, I believe, remained there.

Over the years I have had many requests from my American friends for information concerning Arthur Nash of Tiffany fame, he had a relative who was a neighbour of mine. I have seen and examined three of his signed pieces, all of which he had brought over from America. When I asked which firm he had worked at in Stourbridge, my neighbours were not sure that he had worked in Stourbridge at all. I tried various glassworks and glassworkers' families, but no one had ever heard of him. Thomas Webb's records show that a Charles Nash was the cutting-shop manager in 1893, and during my research I found that an Arthur Nash, a glassworker, had moved from Stratford-on-Avon to Birmingham, and it may be coincidental, but two sisters, named Nash, were working at G. Bacchus & Son of Birmingham when it closed in 1897.

The movement of craftsmen continued, and by this I include employers, because it was unthinkable to have a boss who would not do what he asked his employees to do. The employers also changed partnerships frequently. For some unknown reason the Northern counties and Scotland were often their choice for employment. The reason could have been higher rates of pay to attract their skill.

The next well-known glassman to move was Frederick Carder, chief designer at Stevens & Williams. As a young man he had shown signs of becoming a good artist and was employed as an apprentice at Stevens & Williams in about 1880. John Northwood saw and liked his work and after only a short time Carder became his assistant. Destiny, fate, call it what you will, here was the man to succeed John Northwood and his departure in 1903 for America surprised those who knew him because his family was well respected, but glassworkers, so I was told, (especially those at the works) had expected something to happen. When Mr. Carder left Britain we lost not only a brilliant designer but also a man who could make what he designed. He left in control John Northwood II, a man steeped in glass development since birth, and who was, at that time, quite the equal of Frederick Carder.

There is another point we must consider. Why were so many art treasures made around this date? Tiffany, Locke and Northwood were producing new styles and types, colours and techniques, in many cases by 'hit and miss' methods, and this gave us scores of one-off art pieces. But the market was soon to change. Crystal was the life-blood of the industry and firms were being modernized for more production, and to put it bluntly, did not want to experiment too much. This in my opinion was the position in English glassworks.

The situation in America was somewhat different, for that country was settling down and the people wanted 'nice' things, so artists like Frederick Carder arrived just at the right time to make them. He visited England in 1920 and I understand from his friends he wanted to stay, but he realized he could not fit into the changed conditions. Back in America, he made excellent use of his remaining forty years. As a collector standing on the sidelines, I can see many Stourbridge characteristics in the glass he designed while in America.

But while many of our glass personalities went to America, many preferred their homeland. Until now I have justified the inclusion of an individual because of his above-average manual skill. Actually this is only part of the picture because what was also essential, was a person with the knowledge to co-ordinate these skills for commercial purposes. During the Victorian period many distinguished themselves in the glass trade and in particular, Mr. Wilkes Webb, eldest son of Thomas Webb, founder of Dennis Glass Works, Stourbridge. His father, who died in 1869, had retired four years earlier from the business, but his two sons, Wilkes and Charles, had actually been in charge a few years previous to this time. It was obvious as future events proved, that Wilkes Webb was well informed on the progress of cameo in the district. In 1876 he commissioned John Northwood to make what proved to be his last cameo vase – the Dennis Vase (Pegasus). I was told many times that the cased blank, white over blue, was made at Webb's and that Wilkes himself designed it. The vase was exhibited at the Paris Exhibition of 1878, although it was not finished until 1882; it was sold to Tiffany of New York.

It is fairly certain that Wilkes Webb with his cameo team was only waiting for the 'white-acid' process to be perfected for his semi-commercial cameo to start. This process would, more or less, eliminate hand carving, a very time-consuming operation. I think his organization of all available outworkers was most exemplary. We must dwell a little on this man's ability to organize. The reader may not realize, at first, the significance but when and how he achieved his organization, helps to increase the collector's knowledge.

In those days, 1880–1900, cameo production depended firstly on a perfect cased blank, the fusing of different colours being a very great problem, and one which I believe in some cases resulted in fifty per cent scrap. Because of this difficulty Wilkes Webb contacted chemists for advice, which in turn he put into practice. The next problem was the acid process. This was used to remove, under control, the unwanted parts of a pattern on any glass article to a reasonable depth. The techniques of the job were well understood, but the effects on the operator's hands and arms would not be tolerated today. The third and final operation (unless the articles had to be enamelled) was carried out by engravers whose job it was to elaborate the design and clean up edges and faults which had occurred during the acid process. If Wilkes Webb planned to produce cameo in a big way, he would need more engravers. It would be this part of the scheme where skilled labour was necessary. Engraving is a craft that needs plenty of skill but very little equipment, so it was easy to work at home. In fact this was common practice throughout all glass centres.

It was to these outworkers that Wilkes Webb turned. They could help out if production warranted it. They could also make the 'specials' without disrupting normal output. Now, more than one hundred years after Sir Benjamin Stone first patronized cameo, we may see it again being produced but with modern sophisticated tools.

Another practice of Wilkes Webb and his firm was to name the different styles, such as 'Bronze', 'Burmese' and the 'Flakestone' series, just three of many new styles, and this is another advantage for collectors when classifying.

Occupying a prominent position in the cameo epoch was M. Jules Barbe, Painter, Gilder and Enameller, a personality in his own right. He studied his art in France and arrived in Stourbridge in 1879 where he commenced work at Dennis Glass Works. At the Paris Exhibition of 1878 both Jules Barbe and the firm of Thomas Webb had each exhibited their work. Since their goods were compatible, it was sensible for them to co-operate, which was what they obviously did. It is probable that all had been pre-arranged. In 1900 he left Thomas Webb and started business on his own, and as far as I can ascertain, signed individual pieces only after that date. At the same time my local newspaper said of him, and I quote, 'M. Jules Barbe is generally regarded as the most prominent individual exponent of this art in this country.' This was perhaps a little exaggerated, nevertheless he was a brilliant craftsman.

Another painter, Hugo Maisey (sometimes spelt Mose or Masey) came to Stourbridge from Meistersdorf, Germany in 1912. He became very friendly with Jules Barbe, and a few pieces can be found with both of their signatures. He started work at Webb–Corbett with his daughter as assistant. His work is quite distinctive, as many of his colours have a matt finish. Although working for Webb–Corbett, he obviously decorated for other glassworks as I have some of his pieces with the RD No. 719536–9 'Stuart'.

Pierre Erard, another French artist and friend of Jules Barbe, started the painting and gilding 'shop' for Stevens & Williams around 1885. With him was Arthur Stinton (whose family was connected with the Royal Worcester factory) and third in the team was Mr. Round who worked with copper deposit for gold and silver designs. Later they were joined by Will Capewell who, in his youth, had assisted Jules Barbe. After his retirement Will spent two nights a week trying to explain to me the intricacies of gilding and enamelling. Jules Barbe left Stourbridge in 1925 and died in Switzerland in 1929. Hugo Maisey was interned during the War years on the Isle-of-Man and died in 1932. Arthur Stinton died in the late 1930s aged eighty.

For many collectors I should have mentioned John Thomas Bott earlier, and then in a class of his own. As this book has been designed to help collectors, I feel I must be objective, because, to own an authentic specimen decorated by Thomas Bott is to have an extremely valuable piece. He was born in 1829, trained as a painter at Richardson's, and by 1852 was painting for Worcester Royal Porcelain Works. When he died in 1870 he was Art Director at the Worcester Works. His nephews Tom and George Woodall, expert cameo engravers chiefly employed by Thomas Webb, always appreciated his help.

As I have stated previously, Richardson's record books are few and far between, possibly no more than twelve exist, but in one of them there is reference to a Mr. Lawrence working alongside Mr. Bott. After reading this, many years ago, I made a special effort to find a signed example of Bott's work. Every one of which I

heard, I asked permission to examine, but all were 'attributed' to Bott. The vases themselves can fairly easily be identified as Richardson's, but for collectors I would like more research on the artist. One line of approach would be to compare designs at the Worcester works during Thomas Bott's employment there. This is in no way to discredit Thomas Bott, but to help collectors to identify his work, because today almost any heavy opal vase, decorated with flowers, is claimed to be his work.

During the Victorian period, the glass trade produced hundreds of remarkable personalities from regions other than the Midlands. Some were respected, others tolerated, but all had one ambition, and that was to improve the glass industry. Their operations and achievements stretched from London to the North of Scotland. Some were my friends, some came from families who later helped me to assess their rightful place in glass development, others are shadows I have noted and admired when researching in Patent and Reference Offices.

One such man was Thomas Davidson Esq., J.P. I remember the surprise I had when I found a patent No. 7830 had been granted in 1910 to T. Davidson, Teams Glass Works, Gateshead, for a flower dome, which I thought had been in existence before 1900. (This was a domed glass block pierced with holes, which is placed in a bowl to hold flowers.) I became so impressed with his scores of RD Designs and Patents that I wrote to G. Davidson & Co. for further information about this man, whom I admired but had never met. The firm was founded by George Davidson in 1867. On his father's death in 1891 Thomas took control. Previously the firm's output had been almost entirely pressed glass, but after 1891, baskets, dogs, paperweights and candlesticks were added to their production. After 1922 the whole range of wares was revolutionized with the introduction of hors d'oeuvres plates, trinket sets, coloured flower sets, flower holders, cigarette boxes and ashtrays, made by a process invented by Thomas Davidson. He died in 1937.

To ask anyone with a knowledge of glass history to name a personality from London who influenced the Victorian period, the answer must automatically be James Powell, 1774–1840. With his knowledge and discrete use of colours, together with the practice of employing outside designers, he made, in my opinion, a reputation for Whitefriars. Their designs and output throughout the Victorian period were continuous, and in the best Whitefriars tradition. Besides the essential crystal ware, pale colours were used very cautiously, in many cases added to crystal to emphasize shape.

In 1850 Charles Winston, whose hobby was analysing the colouring agents used for medieval stained glass, approached the firm to test his findings. This was done and resulted in many bright colours in their glassware. There were two reasons why Charles Winston went to James Powell and Sons. Firstly, there had been a revival in the use of stained glass windows, chiefly for churches and manor houses, and Powell's were making sheet glass for this purpose. Secondly, they were always willing to help any artist if they could, and rarely turned anyone away.

To be successful every glassworks must have good designers and first-class workers able to produce the goods. This means co-operation between the glass-blowers and designers and a complete understanding of each others capabilities. Whitefriars would seem to have had these conditions for more than a hundred years. Having an abundance of colour at hand, one would have thought it might be used extravagantly, but this was not so. In fact, to examine some of their museum pieces 1865–7, it comes as a shock to be told that they were made at Whitefriars and not in Venice.

When the Midlands, during the height of the 'fancy' period c. 1880, was being smothered with colour and grotesque shapes, Whitefriars did make a few specimens with applied decorations, but not at all vulgar in colour. The type of glassware with Venetian characteristics had been designed before H. J. Powell took control, but this must have been to his liking, otherwise a much greater change would have taken place, especially as he had colour to hand. Instead he sparingly added tear-drops and threads, with some wheel engraving, a most unusual combination. I do not know of another English firm which used such designs.

Following the death of Harry Powell in 1922, Barnaby Powell became responsible for production which included many styles and types. Barnaby, himself a first-class designer, favoured crystal, but this did not overrule the fact that colour and fashion had to be recognized. Within a few years, a team of men, all specialists in their own areas, were helping to close the Victorian and prepare for the modern or studio periods. These were W. J. Wilson, Art Director, James Hogan, Designer, and Tom Hill, Master Glass Blower. W. J. Wilson who spearheaded the revival of diamond point engraving in this country, was Managing Director and Chief Designer. James Hogan had spent many years at the drawing board at Whitefriars, and Tom Hill came

from Messrs. Walsh, Walsh of Birmingham in 1928. I knew them all, but Tom was a special friend. He learned his trade like his father, at Messrs. Walsh, Walsh and could make almost anything in glass. He helped me with many problems. After the Second World War, I met Mr. Wilson who also helped me a great deal.

I believe we managed to clear up an uncertainty about the London glassware made for Varnish & Co., when the three of us discussed its manufacture. The glassware made for Varnish & Co. is shown and described on pages 98 and 99. This type of glass was acclaimed in Art Journals when registered in 1849, and when exhibited in the Great Exhibition of 1851, it was copied in Germany and America, yet by 1852 its manufacture had ceased. Why?

The general opinion was that it was made at J. Powell & Sons (Whitefriars). I think so too, but there seemed little substantial evidence. I have never liked guess-work, so the obvious move was to go to Whitefriars where Mr. Wilson checked their records and Tom Hill listened to my surmises. Mr. Wilson's search was abortive, he could not find any evidence of his firm making any of this glassware, but Tom Hill came up with the answer to what I believe is the most intriguing question – why had the glass been made for so short a period of time? He convinced me when we went into the glasshouse. Firstly, there were a number of ways to fold the glass back into itself, but only one correct way to get even folded specimens with a minimum number of failures. This was to suck as soon as the blowing operation was completed. The top of the article collapsed into itself, with the rounded edge absolutely free of ripples or corrugations. He showed me other ways to turn the top, but they all tended to distort the edge. After the demonstrations, he suggested why the production of this type of glass was of such short duration. The action of sucking hardened the blower's lungs, because the heat from the article entered the lungs. He remarked that only a fool would make more than one!

Most glassworks make specials, but Whitefriars, during the years that I frequented their works, seemed to encourage their artists to pursue their ideas to their natural conclusion and this resulted in a great number of one-offs. To identify any of these pieces is almost impossible.

Until now we have lionized men who had the advantage of being surrounded by their own countrymen, familiar and ready to assist with any glass-making problem. To this list we must add the name Salvador Ysart, a Continental glass-blower with nothing to offer but his skill. His working life had started uneventfully at the age of nine at a Barcelona glassworks.

In 1909 with his wife and family Ysart emigrated to France and worked in Marseilles and from there he moved to Lyons. He was an individualist, a strict disciplinarian, a perfectionist and a very practical glassworker and, still unsettled, he moved to Choisy-le-Roi on the River Seine, ten kilometres (six miles) from Paris. But in September 1915 he arrived in Scotland and started to work at the Edinburgh and Leith Flint Glass Company, now the Edinburgh Crystal Co. Ltd. In 1922 the family moved to Perth, and Salvador with his four sons, introduced 'Monart Ware' at John Moncrieff Ltd., North British Glassworks, Perth, in 1924. The word 'Monart' is a combination of the two names Moncrieff and Ysart, and as far as I can ascertain this type of decorative glassware had never been made commercially before in the British Isles.

As events proved, John Moncrieff was a very astute business man, he must also have watched and appreciated the development of coloured glass during the latter half of the Victorian period. This is made plain by his interest in and financial backing of a totally unknown type of glassware by an equally unknown glassworker, and a Continental at that! He offered this

to the public in 1924 without any ceremony, at prices much valued by the inhabitants of Perth who purchased specimens for gifts.

I think it is reasonable to assume that John Moncrieff had advance knowledge of the progress being made with this glassware by Salvador Ysart and, possibly, his progress towards Scotland. Whatever the case, it was not difficult to realize that they had the foundation needed to launch and produce an entirely new type of glassware, John in a financial and marketing position, Salvador with an idea and the skill to produce it.

When I first saw 'Monart' in 1930 it was fairly well established as an example of a late Victorian, smooth-type glassware. The Second World War put an end to all decorative glassware, 'Monart' included. In 1945 Salvador and two of his son (one had died) left the North British Glass Works, leaving Paul to restart the manufacture of 'Monart', but Paul's forte was paperweights and it was with these that he became established as one of the world experts. See **229-236** and facing page for remarks concerning this unique glassware. If Salvador Ysart did nothing else, he left behind a type of glassware with a decoration technique which I have noticed is now being frequently used in modern specimens. The reason, it seems, is that it so readily harmonizes with most household colour schemes.

Index to designs 1884–1933

Particulars of designs are included in the official Journal of Patents. The list shows the highest and lowest RD numbers found in each volume. It will be noticed that the numbers overlap somewhat, and it will therefore be necessary in some cases to refer to more than one volume. Glass registration numbers should be under Group III, but occasionally are misprinted under Group IV. The year 1885 is unreliable in this respect.

Readers should remember that the registered number gives the year of registration only. The maker's name can be obtained by making application to a reference library. Present the volume and number and the librarians will give you the information you require.

Volume	Lowest no.	Highest no.
1884 vol. 1	1	8871
1884 vol. 2	8872	18992
1885 vol. 1	18993	28760
1885 vol. 2	28761	39467
1886 vol. 1	38212	51155
1886 vol. 2	47000	64030
1887 vol. 1	61207	75378
1887 vol. 2	66073	89833
1888 vol. 1	87266	102269
1888 vol. 2	96018	116092
1889	111664	140172
1890	139095	163279
1891	160613	184852
1892	180237	204032
1893	201007	224018
1894	221919	246246
1895	233880	267568
1896	257070	290056
1897	285275	310920
1898	302109	330922

Volume	Lowest no.	Highest no.
1899	313829	350675
1900	340826	367634
1901	360834	384489
1902	371435	402112
1903	392760	422997
1904	408651	446801
1905	428004	470855
1906	465328	492874
1907	467274	517524
1908	502933	534104
1909	523477	554717
1910	534174	575662
1911	561570	594079
1912	575100	611522
1913	608541	630059
1914	627492	644783
1915	642613	653479
1916	648264	658961
1917	655001	662792
1918	660812	666065
1919	664587	673595
1920	672154	679607
1921	673026	687002
1922	682114	694916
1923	689308	702544
1924	694509	710040
1925	705943	717905
1926	715706	726269
1927	722887	734263
1928	725899	742656
1929	733667	750966
1930	741336	760435
1931	756794	769489
1932	766526	779110
1933	773751	

Registry or lozenge marks

Various marks of official registration can be found on many glass articles. If all marks are distinct, positive results are obtained.

There are four main avenues of approach for collectors when researching Victorian glass, namely trademarks, two sets of lozenge marks 1842–67 and 1868–83, and RD marks from 1884 until the present day. When first encountered they can seem confusing, but this is not so if the following remarks are noted. The RD numbers (Index to Designs) are by far the most important. The volume in which the required number is recorded states the day, month and year together with the name and address of the firm to which the number was allocated. The word 'design' at times seems misleading because it can mean pattern, shape or colour and the co-operation of the professional staff is necessary if more information is required.

The lozenge mark from either series, until a few years ago, supplied only the registration date but now there is a reference book. Providing the letters and number are correct this will supply the maker's name. To verify the information, a tape can be purchased, and this, when passed through a projector, shows a picture of the specimen allocated to a specific date.

As there are a few official errors (mainly printer's errors) in respect of dates, I have for my own use devised the following procedure. In the 1842–67 series, two errors occur, R and D were used for September 1857, and K and A for December 1860. These errors can really be ignored, as they are of little significance. Likewise in the 1868–83 series W and G were used for March 1878, while D and W were used for the year 1878. There is no problem here as the year letter for the two series falls in different angles, in the top angle for 1842–67 and in the right angle for 1868–83.

Many firms made identification easy by adding their trademark as well as the lozenge mark, but of course the whole exercise becomes useless when the lozenge mark is distorted during manufacture, and this unfortunately was not infrequent.

Class III is, of course, Glass, rather confusing at times when Class IV (Ceramics) is used by mistake.

Years 1842–1867

1842	X	1855	E
1843	H	1856	L
1844	C	1857	K
1845	A	1858	B
1846	I	1859	M
1847	F	1860	Z
1848	U	1861	R
1849	S	1862	O
1850	V	1863	G
1851	P	1864	N
1852	D	1865	W
1853	Y	1866	Q
1854	J	1867	T

Years 1868–1883

1868	X	1876	V
1869	H	1877	P
1870	C	1878	D
1871	A	1879	Y
1872	I	1880	J
1873	F	1881	E
1874	U	1882	L
1875	S	1883	K

Months

January C
February G
March W
April H
May E
June M
July I
August R
September D
October B
November K
December A

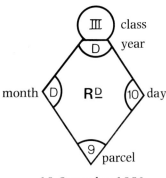

10 September 1852

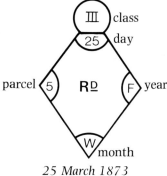

25 March 1873

Glass in colour

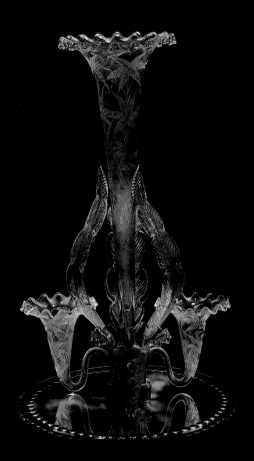

1 This is one of a pair of vases with which I began my glass collection, and therefore it is important to me for sentimental reasons. From the time I bought this vase, I sought to collect Victorian glass in order to establish the development of the various styles made during that period.

Although hundreds of specimens are shown on the following pages, very many more have been destroyed accidentally or thrown away because their shape or colour did not blend with 'modern' decorations as fashions changed. The circumstances of the making of this vase have already been explained, but articles cased yellow over white, which were a speciality of J. F. Bolton Bowater, Platts Glass Works, Amblecote, can be found in shapes other than the one illustrated, bowls, sugars and creams, and even epergnes. The enamel decoration was painted by Kny Bros., The Platts, Amblecote. Designs with birds, like the one shown, have figured on Stourbridge glass for more than a hundred years. 34.3 cm (13½ in) high

2 This vase, one of a set of 3 made by Joseph Locke about 1880, illustrates the technique of enclosing enamelled designs between 2 casings, in this specimen the base colour is pale blue cased with crystal. The impression one gets when the vase is first examined is that the enamelled decoration has been applied direct on to the blue blank before the crystal casing – this is not so! If the vase is turned a little we get a reflection of the design on the blue background, this indicates that a crystal casing was applied over the blue before the design was added, after which a final crystal casing was applied. I cannot see why this extra work was necessary on an already difficult subject, but Locke obviously thought it *was* needed and he seems the only man to have overcome most of the problems during the Victorian period.

Joseph Locke was before my time, but in the early 1920s I talked to many of his contemporaries, who, without exception, spoke of him as the finest glassmaker Stourbridge ever produced. He must also be remembered for producing a replica of the Portland Vase in the incredibly short time of 8 months.

The difficulty of enclosing enamelled subjects, in fact any kind of decoration, was overcome by Orrefors of Sweden. As far back as 1920 they enclosed engravings and called it 'Graal', now they have perfected the technique and are producing fine art pieces. 25.4 cm (10 in) high

3 This is an assembly of birds and flowers around a fountain. To discover the makers and to date it is very difficult, I have seen at least 6 of these articles, and all were identical, including the domes. The structure supporting the birds and branches of leaves and flowers is made from 9.5 mm (⅜ in) diameter drawn crystal rod, much too heavy to be made by the average lampworker (see 5 for more information on lamp-workers).

The 3 white birds, I believe, are Continental, made with the help of a mould and the leaves, too, seem to have been started in a mould. As for the flowers, these could have been made in England but it is very unusual for English lamp-workers to paint their work in this manner. However, the crystal and ruby fountain is typically English, used extensively in the Midlands in particular. Even the white (opal) chain is a different mixture, but it is not an individual item as it has been worked into the main structure. 41.2 cm (16¼ in) high

4 This is an elaborately engraved and rare '6-way' crystal epergne, made by the Amblecote Glass Co., Stourbridge, 1910–20. It is rare because it is so unusual to find one undamaged. It is called a 6-way because it has 3 side trumpets and 3 leaves, the main trumpet is counted only when it forms a single epergne or centre. The top edges of the trumpets are welted – folded under as with a folded foot on a wine.

The leaves are moulded, and finally shaped before cooling. To be correct the trumpets and leaves should be in a glass-fitting on a mirror – should an epergne be found with a brass fitting or its mirror exchanged for a bowl then one can assume that it has been married up after leaving the works. Engraved epergnes were a speciality of the Amblecote Glass Co., who, I believe, took over from Joseph Fleming & Co., established in 1889. 66 cm (26 in) high

5 This glass ship is one of the hundreds made during the Victorian period. They vary in size considerably, from 15–60 cm (6–24 in) in height is the general range, but sometimes a 'special' was made, a little taller. Colour-wise, we get a variation; crystal often, but they always seem insipid. Red, white, and blue are the most common colours, yellow and brown occasionally. A well-made, reasonable-size specimen with these colours is very attractive and desirable for the collector to have. Even as a boy these ships attracted me. I saw many varieties for they were fairly common in homes at the turn of the century. Noting my interest, my parents, who had seen them made, were able to explain their manufacture.

A number of things they explained at that time I did not understand, but many years later their detailed explanation helped me to research the origin of these ornaments. The results I hope will help collectors, and to a large extent, explain some of the controversial points which have arisen over the years.

I discovered that some 75% of the ships were made by travelling craftsmen, but the domes were made by a few glassworks around the country. In the Midlands G. Bacchus and Sons, Birmingham, made domes in many shapes and sizes which they sold from the works, not only to glassworkers, but to taxidermists and wax flower artists.

The glassman's (lamp-worker) tools consisted of a handcart with two wheels at the rear and one let in front, together with a spirit-blowpipe or bunsen, foot-blower, sticks of glass, both crystal and coloured, and a number of domes and bases in a number of sizes, and of course his personal tools. One thing worried me! How did the travelling lamp-worker generate enough heat to melt the glass rods? Some time later I found on a market stall, an old book 'Glass Working by heat and by abrasion', edited by Paul N. Hasluck, Cassell & Co. Ltd., London, 1899, and this book gives at least 6 ways to make a spirit-blowpipe or bunsen suitable for lamp work.

When a glassman arrived in any town the procedure was always the same. He looked for a house whose owner he thought might have a few shillings to spare, and would suggest he made them a ship for whatever cash they had to spare. The price agreed varied from 2 to 21 shillings (10p to 105p or a guinea). A guinea ship would cause great excitement for the children who always crowded around him, knowing he would be there for 3 or 4 days. His sleeping accommodation was generally solved when he was offered the garden shed with straw to rest his body.

When the ship was finished, the children could always tell how well the glassman had been treated by how elaborately it was finished, such as the number of sailors in the rigging, and the number of small ships including around the main vessel.

I attempted to trace about 20 back to source and every one led to St. Helens. The one illustrated was bought from a house in St. Helens. It seems obvious to me that these travelling lamp-workers, were taught their trade at St. Helens, possibly there was a family of lamp-workers around there. A similar example is that of the Glass Toy Makers of Birmingham, these men need not have been trained glass-blowers, in fact they could have learned their trade at home.

All this raises the question as to whether these ships were ever made commercially. If this means by the hundred and sold wholesale, the answer must be no. Had a glassworks wanted a few 'specials' or one for commemorative purposes these would have been made by outworkers, as lamp-workers were seldom directly employed. Popularity for this type of lamp work reached its peak around 1875. 53.3 cm (21 in) high.

6   7   8   9   10

11   12   13   14   15

16   17   18   19   20

6 Signed 'Richardson Vitrified Enamel Color', registered in 1847. By no means the earliest Victorian glass recorded, and in fair supply. The decoration is an Egyptian scene, used extensively on the early pieces. Later, English rural scenes and floral designs in colour were introduced. These jugs are rather heavy, and rank as some of the art pieces of the period. 24.1 cm ($9\frac{1}{2}$ in) high

7 A goblet from the same period as the previous jug, signed 'Richardson Vitrified Enamel Color'. The decoration is as for 6. 16.5 cm ($6\frac{1}{2}$ in) high

8 A green jug of Richardson's vitrified series, which although not signed, is genuine. It was finished, like 9, too late for the Great Exhibition of 1851. 20.3 cm (8 in) high

9 A green fruit dish. Signed 'Richardson Vitrified Enamel Color' registered in 1852. Not decorated – Richardson's believed that plain designs could be as attractive as enamelled pieces. Like the matt-finished opal specimens 6 and 7 the green pieces are rather heavy in weight. 21.6 cm ($8\frac{1}{2}$ in) diameter

10 Another example of Richardson's vitrified, one of a pair of vases both signed. Only the outer surface is matt finished, to help the decorator. The opal is unusually clear, but in many pieces the potash is not completely dissolved. 17.1 cm ($6\frac{3}{4}$ in) high

11 An early specimen of Richardson's alabaster, all the decoration hand-painted, genuine, but unsigned. Size for size, it is heavier than vitrified due, I think, to an increase of lead in the glass batch. This type of vase could be as early as 1855. 20.3 cm (8 in) high

12 A much later alabaster vase, hand painted after being line drawn. Very heavy. Signed 'Richardson's Stourbridge'. One from a set of 3, c. 1860 onwards, 25.4 cm (10 in) high

13 One of a pair of exquisitely decorated alabaster vases, an unusual Stourbridge shape, obviously designed to suit the decoration which is expertly painted on a primrose background, heavy and signed 'Richardson's Stourbridge' c. 1860. 17.8 cm (7 in) high

14 One of a pair of Richardson's alabaster vases with a typical French top, rather unusual for such a traditional firm. I queried this type of design in the early 1920s and was told that a number of French men and women worked at the factory around 1870. The coloured pellets I traced to Birmingham where there used to be a thriving trade in what was then called 'Glass Toys'. Richardson's probably used more glass pellets than any other Stourbridge glassworks. 31.8 cm ($12\frac{1}{2}$ in) high

15 One of a pair of Richardson's alabaster lustres, once again coloured pellets have been freely used to emphasize the opal. These pendants are fairly certain to have been made by F. & C. Osler, Birmingham, c. 1890. 27.9 cm (11 in) high

16 A cased vase, iridescent crystal over opal. Made at Richardson's, the first of a series. In the trade this ware was loosely called opal iridescent, but with the records lost I call it 'pearl button glass'. It was also made in a large size, a semi-commercial product. Other oddly shaped vases are occasionally found, c. 1900. 16.5 cm ($6\frac{1}{2}$ in) high

17 A small rectangular, deep fruit dish tinted green before being shaped but could be any colour. A development of 16 with the same mixture, iridescent cased crystal over opal, c. 1900. 26 cm ($10\frac{1}{4}$ in) long

18 An oval flower bowl with hand applied green threads and folded, pinched top. A further development with the same mixture, iridescent cased crystal over opal, may be found with different coloured threads, c. 1900. 15.9 cm ($6\frac{1}{4}$ in) long

19 A flower vase made from the same mixture and cased in the same manner as the 3 previous specimens. The pattern is mould blown, then transferred to a punty-iron to form the top and apply the green drops. This method of applying drops was common practice at Richardson's. Other firms generally reversed them, leaving the tails hanging down. A somewhat similar vase was produced on the Continent but with a difference. The shape, size and surface pattern are almost identical, but the Continental specimen although mould blown, has no punty mark, no drops, is not crystal cased and is only half the weight. c. 1900. 12 cm ($4\frac{3}{4}$ in) high

20 Another vase from the same group, a very poor specimen little better than its Continental counterpart. The only visible difference is that the English version is crystal cased, thus being a little heavier. c. 1900. 16.5 cm ($6\frac{1}{2}$ in) high

21 One of a pair of Bohemian-type vases made by Richardson's, c. 1880, cased opal over ruby and crystal. This sounds contrary and may be controversial so an explanation is given on page 32. 27.9 cm (11 in) high

22 Another Richardson's copy of a Bohemian, but much easier to imitate. The jug which is cased white (opal) over crystal is not so skilfully made as its Bohemian counterpart. The foot is clumsy and the gilding uneven. Probably a little earlier than 1880. 33 cm (13 in) high

23 A simple cased vase made by Richardson's when they and G. Bacchus of Birmingham accepted the German challenge on cased glass after the Great Exhibition, 1851. Many sizes, in simple shapes, were made by the hundred, with 3 and sometimes 4 casings, and many trial colours, invariably starting with crystal on the inside. This one is white over ruby over crystal. The dates range from before 1860 to 1900. 19.7 cm (7¾ in) high

24 A Richardson snake-handled jug, an example of cased alabaster. Note the French influence in the use of the snake. These are not plentiful, but vary a great deal in colour. I have only seen this type of jug in this size and occasionally the casing is omitted. c. 1890. 30.5 cm (12 in) high

25 A lustre, cased white over ruby over crystal, with 10 pendants, made at Richardson's. I believe the pendants were at first made there but later at Oslers. They are difficult to match as the stem varies in length and design. Although they have a Bohemian look they are much heavier than any I have seen, 1890–1900. 34.3 cm (13½ in) high

26 Bottles like this one were made at Richardson's by the hundred, shape and height varied little, but colour, casing and types of decoration were almost too numerous to imagine. They were made chiefly to contain liqueurs or wines, singly as shown, but often in 3s, enamelled with Rum, Gin, etc. Others had figures in monochrome obviously the worse for drink. The most valuable are signed 'Richardson Vitrified'. Stoppers were often ordinary cork, but also solid or hollow glass ones were made. 1870–1900. 36.8 cm (14½ in) high

27 Two-coloured cameo brandy flask, ruby over opal opalescent made by Richardson's a little after 1900, a commercial product. The shape was used extensively by the firm for many glass mixtures. 15.2 cm (6 in) high

28 An ingenious, effective and cheap commercial way to produce cameo. It was designed to use ordinary cutting wheels, releasing engravers for more intricate work. The date about 1880 because the makers, Richardson's, used the same mixture of opal as used on 21 and 22. 30.5 cm (12 in) high

29 A most interesting piece of cameo, obviously experimental, or one of a few. Supposed to be Richardson's, but I do not think so. The blank green over pale ivory I feel sure was made at Thomas Webb, Amblecote, while the decoration ('A Lion Eating its Prey') in monochrome was finished at John Northwood's works at Wordsley. It is far from being a saleable commodity, because most of the green casing had to be removed, leaving only the design outlines, which is rather small for the large surface area. For it to be John Northwood's work it must be before 1900 as John died in 1902. Rather a mystery piece. 28.6 cm (11¼ in) high

30 A piece of commercial cameo, a decanter cased blue over citrine over crystal. Made at Richardson's after 1900, nicely designed, but very different from other Stourbridge cameo. Perhaps the vine pattern is too intricate. 25.4 cm (10 in) high

31 Specimens decorated only with cutting are not generally accepted as collectors' items, but there are exceptions. Illustrated is a piece that must be considered if only for the skill required to produce it. In the first place it is long and weighty, secondly any hesitation by the operator will show, especially as the vase is cased white over green, but a far greater problem is that it has to be cut under the wheel instead of over, for this is the only way the cutter can sense direction. His machine would be in first-class condition, a very important point as we are talking about 80 years ago. Being made at Richardson's would account for all these problems being surmounted. 39.4 cm (15½ in) high

32 One of a pair of opal vases made at Richardson's c. 1900. With a minimum amount of design and colour, an awkward shape becomes superb. 24.8 cm (9⅞ in) high

33 A very early jug signed 'Richardson 1854'. I am not sure what was registered, the spout formation, the rope handle, or the decoration, but most likely the latter. Many years later John Northwood used it and it continued to be used at his works until 1918. It was a very time-consuming operation, all the pattern marks are hand-worked, and only girls with the right temperament could do the job. Richardson's used this form of decoration on their Bohemian-type overlay specimens. 27.3 cm (10¾ in) high

34 A table centre in alabaster, 2 colours, opal and green, matt-finished on the outside. Made at Richardson's in a number of sizes, but I have only seen them in white and green. They proved very popular in the U.S. The date is a problem as they were made in batches to order, both before and after 1900. 40.6 cm (16 in) high

35 Vases of this type were sold for many years as French in many parts of the country, especially London. About 20 years ago a lot of similar but broken vases were found in a field belonging to Richardson's and since then the peculiar brick colour and archer design have also been found on other vases made by the firm. There is very little evidence on which to date these vases but it must be well before 1900. 36.2 cm (14¼ in) high

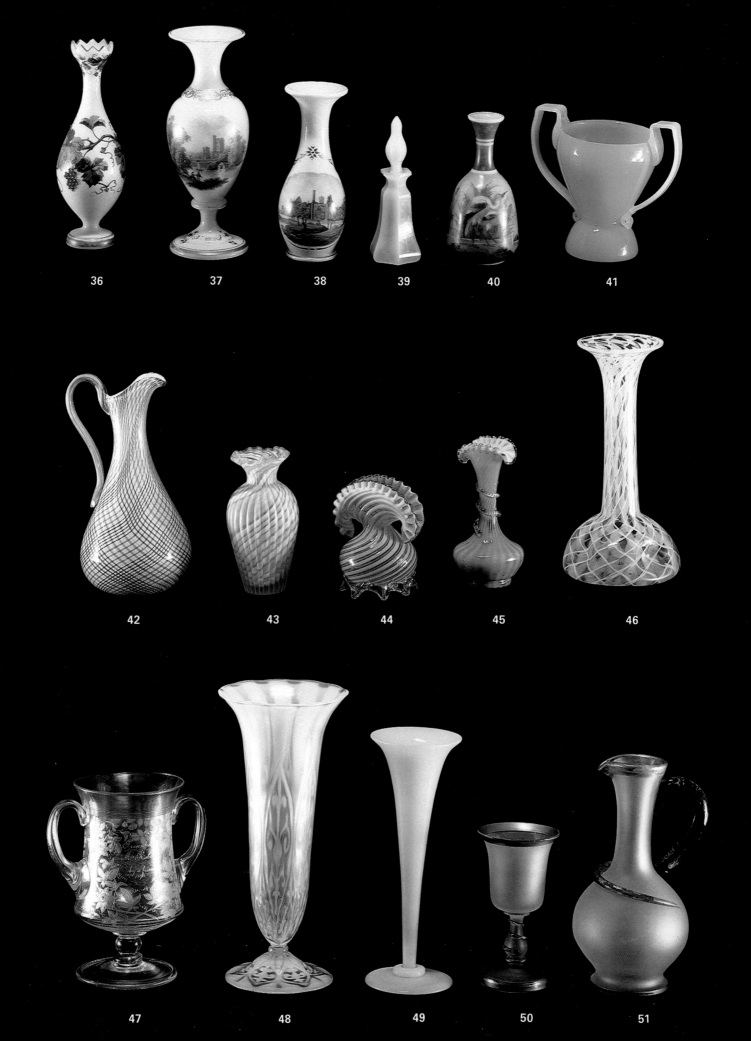

36   37   38   39   40   41

42   43   44   45   46

47   48   49   50   51

36 A Richardson's alabaster vase (one of a pair) showing a design incorporating painting and glass pellets which suggests that their early glass included a number of French innovations, in this case, the rim formation – English ground rims are rare. c. 1880. 25.7 cm (10½ in) high

37 This specimen is in the same category as **38**. Both were made by Richardson's, but there are a number of differences. This vase is alabaster and perhaps a little earlier than **38**, c. 1880. It is one of their regular shapes, the gilt pattern on the neck and foot quite common. The scene is very detailed with no strong outlines which suggests it was done outside the works, as most of their designs were classical with clear lines and painted or enamelled. The picture though pleasant is not professional, neither is it signed. 27.9 cm (11 in) high

38 It was common practice during the Victorian period for glassworks to make blanks for amateur artists to decorate which were then handed back for the picture to be muffled (fixed). On most pieces the gilt work which generally surrounds the painting has been applied at the works professionally. This vase is entitled 'Christchurch, Hants' and signed T. Fall. 21.6 cm (8½ in) high

39 Alabaster perfume bottles, both plain and decorated, were made by Richardson's for many years after 1870. A plain example looks superb, the shape showing a perfect balance, but with decorations added it becomes little more than a fairground gift. 18.4 cm (7¼ in) high

40 Illustrated is a vase, but as some examples had stoppers, could they double-up as perfume bottles? This is only a guess and as they are quite large, I may be wrong. Richardson's c. 1900. 18.4 cm (7¼ in) high

41 This specimen may not impress some collectors, but it would need a first-class glass-blower to make it. Two thinly shaped strap handles on a very heavy body, coupled with 2 different mixtures – not a job for an apprentice. The handle is cracked where it joins the body, because the worker allowed his pinchers to cool. c. 1900. 18.4 cm (7¼ in) high

42 A Richardson's jug manufactured basically as **43**, but in this case latticinio or filigree canes have been added, making it possibly one of the finest examples ever produced in England. There are 3 casings, the inside white, next the casing containing the canes and finally the crystal layer. I do not think they were made in quantity as I have only seen one other. I call it 'Gingham' ware as it is so like the material of that name. 27.9 cm (11 in) high

43 To make this vase, the blue and white canes are placed in a vertical mould in equally spaced grooves, then a gathering of crystal is pressed into and around them which allows the canes to be pulled from the mould. A few blows down the pipe and the canes can be marvered into the crystal body. A punty-iron is pressed on to the base and twisted, an action that angles the canes which by now are only colours worked into the glass. The punty-iron is removed and the vase is blown in a pillar mould to form the vertical ribs. Then it is back on to the punty-iron to form the top. Stevens & Williams, for more details see page 32. 19 cm (7½ in) high

44 One of a pair, and a most intriguing specimen, an example of glassware where Continental and English pieces *look* identical, for more details see page 17. This Richardson vase was made with a lead mixture and is very heavy. It was blown in a ribbed mould, the angle of the ribs formed as for **43**, and then worked entirely on the pontil. The opalescent effect is obtained by slightly cooling the article, then holding it in front of the glory-hole, the heat from which plays on all raised parts, which turn white. This same effect can be obtained with cold air, but it is not so easy an operation. 14.6 cm (5¾ in) high

45 This is a Richardson cased vase, blue over white, with crystal snake, somewhat like **44**. The appearance is good, although the effects have been achieved in a cheaper manner. The lower half is mould blown, after the casing operation. The mould has ribs which are shallow without sharp edges, and with the blowing which follows, the extra metal in the grooves is obviously thicker, thus we get 2 shades of blue. 17.8 cm (7 in) high

46 A crystal commercial vase decorated with white filigree worked into the glass. The haphazard application of white blotches is, I think, a crude way to make poorly applied cane saleable. This is an unusual piece for Richardson's but there were times when some goods fell a little below their high standard. 29.8 cm (11¾ in) high

47 This is an example of crystal and colour combined although the only colour used is 20 or so brown threads emphasizing the top of this 2-handled vase. They were made, as far as I can tell, by Richardson's in 3 sizes – **47** is the middle size – and were all intended as commemorative pieces. The wording and decoration differs on each one, and the date is generally included, this one being 1895. As each is a 'one-off' the collector should never hesitate to acquire one. 24.1 cm (9½ in) high

48 This vase may not impress many readers, but it is very important to a collector because of the skill needed to obtain the opalescent effects. Re-heating glass articles made with certain mixtures turns them white, so if the article has a raised pattern and heat is applied gently, only the pattern changes colour. This is what happened at first to this vase, the glass-blower still had to obtain the vertical patches which start at the rim and fade away downwards and he used a mask with slots hanging from the rim of the vase. The mould for this vase should be with Thomas Webb, because they bought it from Richardson's in the early 1930s. c. 1900. 35.6 cm (14 in) high

49 A simply-shaped vase, common to almost every glassworks in England. It is included here as an example of Richardson's Yellow – each glassworks had its own colours which acted almost as a trademark. 30.5 cm (12 in) high

50 & 51 A very early Victorian goblet and water jug. Although showing signs of wear, the tell-tale marks of careful workmanship are evident. A mark has been ground around the top and spout for the gilding limit and the top is not only shaped but also polished. The outer surface has been matt-finished by hand. They are very heavy and must be earlier than 1850. 19 cm (7½ in) & 28.6 cm (11¼ in) high

52   53   54   55   56

57   58   59   60

61   62   63   64

52 An example of machine-threaded ware, made by Stevens & Williams in 1886, RD 55693. The colour shown is not consistent with other specimens, but this colour is the most plentiful. Other pieces were made in ruby and crystal. 24.1 cm (9½ in) high

53 This is a development of example **52**. The threads of primrose and blue are applied to a crystal bowl, and it is the colour of the threads that gives the impression of 3-colour work. The pinch-work feet and band are applied crystal. The top is formed by pressing the bowl on to fixed bars to get whatever formation is required. 19.7 cm (7¾ in) diameter

54 This Czechoslovak specimen is for comparison of style with the decanter (**52**). The threads have been applied by hand on a cheap colourful vase, c. 1926. 14.6 cm (5¾ in) high

55 A further development. The threads are applied as before, and can be pulled into any shape with a comb or a pointed wire. In this case, the result is called 'pull ups'. The threads are then pressed into the body of the bowl on a marver. The bowl or centre is 2 layers or casings. The top formation is made in the same way as **53**. 15.2 cm (6 in) diameter

56 This is another cased vase, ruby over pink, with applied crystal feet on 'pull up' threaded work. This is the beginning of applied decorations on threaded specimens. 21.6 cm (8½ in) high

57 This is an example of distorting the threads to form clouds. By added decorations of powdered gold and oxides of various colours to fill in the pattern, the beautiful type of glassware registered as 'Tapestry' was made in 1886. 17.1 cm (6¾ in) high

58 A very early piece of applied ware made before John Northwood worked at Stevens & Williams. The vase is a little unusual, it is cased with the first layer being tinted with their old cherry red, over white. The applied flowers are carnations, hand-made the old way. The feet are damaged slightly, but with a specimen so rare and old, the collector has no choice. c. 1860–70. 33 cm (13 in) high

59 The flower formation on this vase started the development of further designs, the applied 3 feet being part of the floral design. RD 15353 in 1884. 20.3 cm (8 in) high

60 This centre bowl with Matsu-No-Ke decoration should be studied by all collectors as it has so many of Stevens & Williams's characteristics. Note the applied flowers (mould-made), the feet and leaves forming a pattern, the 3 feet design, and the top. It is one of John Northwood's own designs, and is signed 'B & Co. Ltd.' and is cased in shaded cherry red over white. 15.2 cm (6 in) high

61 This is not an exquisite specimen, but it helps the collector to follow the development of the applied style. These mistletoe vases are not plentiful, but some of the larger ones, well covered with berries, are magnificent. This example can be dated around 1887. 15.9 cm (6¼ in) high

62 Another centre bowl, a little mixture of old and new methods. The top is hand-formed, the feet a much later design, application of the plums is poor because the stems are too long, also the pale ruby body lacks depth of colour. c. 1887. 15.2 cm (6 in) high

63 A Richardson specimen, a much earlier piece than I thought when I acquired it. The body is their early citrine, and the lizard is hand-made. Notice the 4 stubby feet and blurred edges. c. 1870. 29.2 cm (11½ in) high

64 An unusual vase, the body crystal over pale amethyst with silver fleck (aventurine) between applied crystal lizards. I think Frederick Carder did a little designing here! c. 1900. 15.2 cm (6 in) long

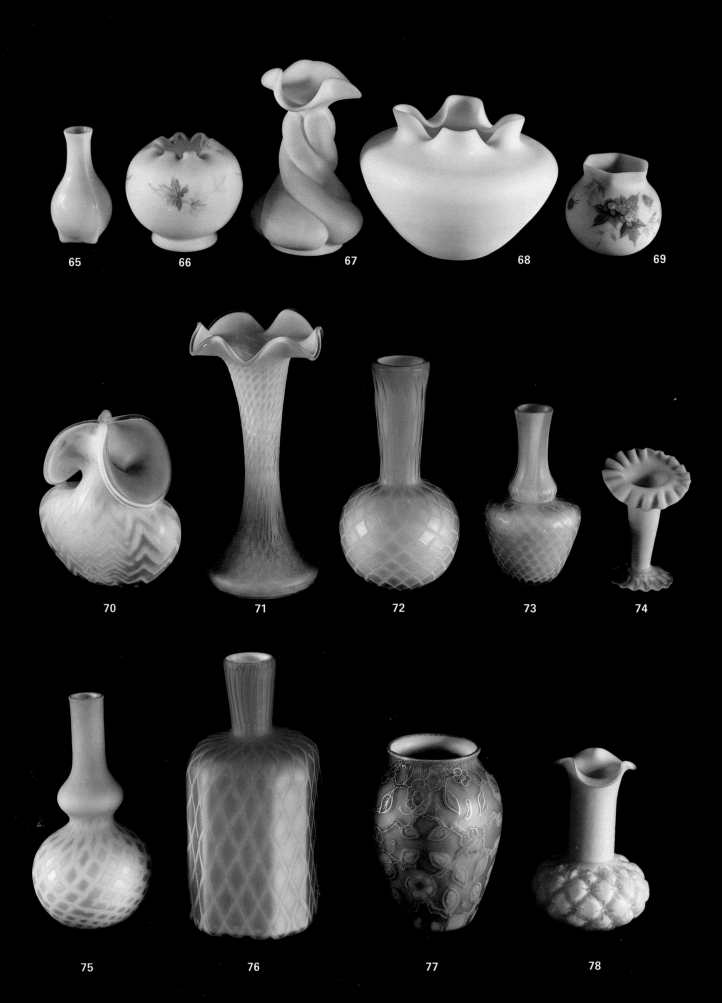

65   66   67   68   69

70   71   72   73   74

75   76   77   78

65 An experimental piece, the intention was to blow the bottom section in a mould, apply the iron and work a wavy top, pink only on the inside, but to reflect through the cream exterior. The top gave too much trouble so it was cut off. A fair number are to be found. Signed Thomas Webb, c. 1900. 9 cm ($3\frac{5}{8}$ in) high

66 A 'Burmese' reproduction from the U.S.A., moulded and decorated by The Fenton Art Glass Co., West Virginia, c. 1974. 10.2 cm (4 in) diameter

67 This is an example of 'Burmese' which I hope will help English collectors. It is moulded, and I have always thought it to be made at Gundersen–Pairpoint Glass Works, New Bedford, Massachusetts in the 1950s. 10.2 cm (4 in) diameter

68 An example of signed 'Queen's Burmese'. The colour is pale with only a small amount of pink, very noticeable in many signed pieces during the early period of this glass. Thomas Webb, c. 1888. 17.8 cm (7 in) diameter

69 A piece of Thomas Webb's 'Burmese'. The design is almost a trademark, the colour is very rich, an alteration made by Webb's after purchasing the glass mixture recipe from the U.S.A. c. 1900–20. 7.6 cm (3 in) high

70 A specimen of Stevens & Williams 'Satin' glass. Note the pattern and shape. Together they give the manufacturer's name and date. It is cased crystal over opal over matt ruby, c. 1900. 12.7 cm (5 in) high

71 Bohemian-made to compete with English and American Satin. It is cased very thin and coloured at the top, outside only, the pattern is moulded in a very clever way, vertical ribs, crossed by angled ones. The date is pre-1914. 21.6 cm ($8\frac{1}{2}$ in) high

72 A first-class example of Satin cased blue over white and finally crystal to show up the pattern. Thomas Webb, c. 1870. 17.8 cm (7 in) high

73 An example of 'Rainbow Satin' at one time thought to be the perfection of Satin ware. Thomas Webb, c. 1880. 14 cm ($5\frac{1}{2}$ in) high

74 A controversial specimen. It was made as 'Blue Burmese', Satin finished, so to English glassmakers it was blue Satin. The word Satin to English glassworkers is a type of finish, while in the U.S.A., collectors mean M.O.P. or Mother-of-Pearl. Thomas Webb, c. 1900. 10.2 cm (4 in) high

75 Another example of Satin, cased red over white, and with air traps reversed. Made in 3 shapes and a number of colours, they were made with 1, 2 or 3 blown rings in the neck and have a ground flat top. This type of finish is very uncommon in English glasshouses. Thomas Webb, c. 1900. 19 cm ($7\frac{1}{2}$ in) high

76 A very heavy, cased, blue over white Satin vase. Made in 2 sizes by Richardson's. When Richardson's closed, Thomas Webb bought their moulds, so some vases could still be made from them. c. 1900. 21.6 cm ($8\frac{1}{2}$ in) high

77 The ultimate in Satin known as 'Platinized Satin'. It is cased, the outer case being dichroic over white, it has a shallow cameo design all over. Thomas Webb, c. 1900. 14.6 cm ($5\frac{3}{4}$ in) high

78 Satin became too expensive to make, and as usual, something cheaper, with good looks, had to be found. This vase was the result. It is single and self-coloured, blown in a mould to form the pattern on the bottom half, and the top formed on the pontil. Thomas Webb, c. 1900. 13.3 cm ($5\frac{1}{4}$ in) high

79   80   81   82   83

84   85   86   87   88   89   90

91   92   93

79 One of a pair of threaded crystal vases; a mundane, very commercial one, made in larger numbers than the earlier specimens. These are found with ordinary crystal feet as well as the mirror type. It is recorded that some were produced with coloured threads. Note the way the twisted band on the stem is formed. This can help in identification as certain shapes are constant with types, in many cases common to a particular glassworks. Stevens & Williams. 11.4 cm (4½ in) high

80 Another commercial piece of threaded ware, a little earlier than **79**, c. 1895. It was made in fairly large numbers and carries the RD 55693. This is an example of threading over pillar moulding. The top is one of John Northwood's semi-automatically shaped tops. Stevens & Williams. 12.7 cm (5 in) diameter

81 This specimen is a much better type than **79** both in skill and value. The article itself has diamond air traps worked into the glass, a raspberry prunt covers the punty mark, finished off with 3 crystal snail feet, Stevens & Williams, c. 1890. 20.3 cm (8 in) diameter

82 This and the previous 2 examples show what can be achieved when colour and shape are manipulated. All 3 come under RD 55693, and although the glass mixture is the same it is because the shape and thickness vary that the 3 pieces take on different shades. This, as with the last specimen, is finished off with a raspberry prunt and 3 crystal snail feet. Stevens & Williams. 21.6 cm (8½ in) diameter

83 Oil and vinegars were at one time common table utensils during Victorian times, but before the end of the century had become little more than ornaments. Checking their history, they seemed to have been very much in use in the Latin countries as early as the 17th century. Many glassworks in England made them in one form or another, but as far as I can ascertain, only Stevens & Williams threaded them. As yet they are only a curiosity but I think they are worth collecting. 11.4 cm (4½ in) high

84–90 These specimens were all made by Stevens & Williams between the wars. As they are termed alabaster, we, as collectors want to know why, because of the Richardson's wares of the same name. I have put this question to scores of glassworkers, and the answer has always been, 'It's opal.' It seems that all white glass, as far as they are concerned, is opal, although they do remark on the fact that some opal mixtures 'work' better than others.

What is the official definition of alabaster? It is a mineral, and occurs in nature as a soft white rock, sometimes having red and yellow shades, sometimes opalescent, pearly or matt, so we can assume it to be a special opal mixture particular to any firm. Richardson's added colour occasionally, but varied the lead content to facilitate certain shapes. Stevens & Williams aimed at translucency which caused Frederick Carder problems when he made his alabaster in the U.S.A. More about this on page 31. For dating purposes, as Richardson's alabaster closely followed their vitrified, this being officially 1847, the first specimens must have been around 1850. I am not sure about Stevens & Williams's earliest, but I do know of some cased vases of Rose-du-Barry (alabaster) which had been decorated by John Northwood's decorating firm, so it would be after 1860. On the other hand, they continued its manufacture until 1938, another example of the duration of the 'Victorian Period'. As will be seen from the illustrations, their products depended on colours and shapes, whereas Richardson's used various surface decorations. Note the translucency of all applied parts.

84: Rose-du-Barry with alabaster handle and foot, 5.7 cm (2¼ in) high. **85:** orange vase on alabaster foot, 10.8 cm (4¼ in) high. **86:** blue with alabaster foot, 24.1 cm (9½ in) high. **87:** Rose-du-Barry with alabaster foot, 26 cm (10¼ in) high. **88:** a sugar (jade) with alabaster stem and foot, 12 cm (4¾ in) high. **89:** blue powder bowl with knop and foot of alabaster, 10.2 cm (4 in) diameter. **90:** pale green powder bowl with alabaster knop and foot, 10.2 cm (4 in) diameter.

91 This and **92** are 2 examples of Stevens & Williams 'Caerleon', the first a vase and the second a jug. I have only recently been able to identify this type of glassware. The name is official, and for some time I have been trying to connect the name with the glass, and I find there must be some linkage with King Arthur because Caerleon was one of his major towns. The glass itself is a soda-lime crystal. Coloured powdered glass has been worked into the surface to a depth of 1.6 mm (1/16 in), making it appear as a casing. The 3 leaves were suggested by John Northwood II, the upper surface of them being iridescent. I understand that this formation of leaves was used on other types of glassware, another fact to be remembered. 22.9 cm (9 in) diameter

92 This example of 'Caerleon' seems to have more connection with King Arthur since there are 2 prunts of his 'face', one on the handle base, and one on the centre of the jug. The surface is different from the previous specimen as the applied powder is made up of much larger particles together with a few bubbles. The date for both specimens is 1927–31. 21.6 cm (8½ in) diameter

93 This type of glassware made by Stevens & Williams is one of the few shapes which can be used to identify a specific variety. It is ribbed Rockingham cased crystal with silver flecks (aventurine). I have seen these in 2 sizes, but have reason to believe there are others. It is my opinion that this type was the forerunner of the unique 'Silveria', see page 33. 25.4 cm (10 in) high

94

95

96

97

98

99

100

101

102

103

104

105

The following 6 pieces are of exceptional interest because they provide a great deal of information essential to any serious collector. Price-wise they are reasonable, but more important, specimens like these are waiting to be recognized.

94 Since I cannot illustrate an example of 'Silveria', a paperweight made in the same colours and style is shown. The actual specimens vary considerably in shape and size, but the colours are constant. The silver fleck, however, can range from that shown to silver foil, the surface can be rough or smooth. Stevens & Williams, I believe the only maker, c. 1900. 7 cm (2¾ in) diameter

95 This is 3-cased, crystal over pale ruby, over white, with Stevens & Williams's usual silver fleck. Take particular note of the shape, which very occasionally is found on Continental glass, but lacks the weight of the English specimen. The folded top is almost a trademark of Stevens & Williams but with the added 3 casings, fleck and ground out pontil, it is certain that it was made by the firm. 13.3 cm (5¼ in) long

96 Another Stevens & Williams example, the top varies slightly compared with **95**, but the 36 ribs decide its origin, the firm used ribbed moulds more than any other English firm. Although significant, the number of ribs could vary, but with more of their characteristics present this is not too important. It is crystal over white, but what is outstanding is that the inner white blank is splashed with ruby on the inside only, while the outside has yellow, blue and ruby markings. 13.3 cm (5¼ in) high

97 An example of splashed glass which I think was made at Boulton & Mills, Audnam Glass Works. I knew the firm well, the workmen were as good as any in the Stourbridge district. Their crystal glass was superb, it was sold as silver crystal and even in a crystal district was held in high esteem, but their coloured wares always puzzled me. When they closed down in the 1920s I bought some of their coloured glass, and it so resembled that made by other firms I always thought it had been bought in. Anyway the characteristics of this vase are so Stourbridge, I will point out some of them.
    Splashed ware was rarely used on art glass, but if used at all was chiefly in pastel

shades. The controversial points are the shape of the top, the excessive wavy outline and a cup, much too large, balanced on a narrow neck. These are typically Continental, but the rest of the vase is very Stourbridge – colour, weight, dense casings, and above all a solid English foot. 17.1 cm (6¾ in) high

98 A small cased bowl, brown over white, over pale blue. The gold decoration was painted by either Pierre Erard, or Jules Barbe, but Pierre Erard the more likely because of the date 1890. Note the distinctive shape of the top, Stevens & Williams 'trademark'. 9.5 cm (3¾ in) diameter

99 One of a pair of jug-shaped satin vases, pale yellow over white, made the Continental way in a mould. No pontil, blown from the top and ground off. The handle a little heavier than foreign glass-blowers make, but the pattern gives it away. Most unusual for Stevens & Williams, c. 1910. 15.9 cm (6¼ in) high

100 The following 3 are all experimental pieces made at Stevens & Williams by Frederick Carder, c. 1900. He either made them or supervised their making. After experimenting, he invariably left the pieces lying around the factory. What he was aiming at with these 3 specimens I can only guess. **100** is a cased jug, crystal over opal with a little ruby worked into the top. The marks on the body look like a type of 'Peloton' ware, which is coloured broken threads marvered into the surface before being cased with crystal. In this case he replaced coloured threads with opal, possibly to see the effect after applying the crystal casing. 14.6 cm (5¾ in) high

101 As I have never seen this kind of decoration on Stevens & Williams's alabaster, I can only assume that Carder had Tiffany in mind. The bowl is pale green on an alabaster foot, the decoration is brown threads worked into the glass itself. This may seem commonplace, but in his case the threads leave and re-enter the bowl, continuing the pattern. Real skill, but suitable only for art pieces. 21.6 cm (8½ in) diameter

102 I cannot see anything unusual in this jug but there must be something, somewhere. The claw handle is not uncommon. In 1900 there was (and still is) a Bohemian glass, being sold in Britain, in scores of different shapes, yellow with white markings cased with thin crystal. Could it be that he wanted to show how it should be made? See **442**. 15.2 cm (6 in) high

103 Another example of a Stevens & Williams rib mould. It is ruby and white cane worked into white, cased with crystal, blown in a rib mould and finished with a ribbed claw handle. A few years before 1900. 19.7 cm (7¾ in) high

104 A fine example of 'Peloton' ware. This type of glass was originally German and I believe it to be copied by the English which in itself is unusual. It was made in Stourbridge, but I have been unable to trace the manufacturer. This is strange because salt cellars in this ware are fairly common. The broken threads are either marvered into the body or scattered on the surface. Some are single colours to contrast with the background or mixed as shown. Thomas Webb made a variety of salts in this ware before 1900, but as far as I can ascertain no art pieces. It is very heavy and has been repaired, a fault which I overlook on rare pieces. On the evidence I have it could be Boulton & Mills, c. 1900 or Thomas Webb's 'Vermacilly' c. 1860. See **441** for an example of the German type. 23.5 cm (9¼ in) high

105 No doubt who made this vase. Applied crystal over ruby, skill and colour excellent – Stevens & Williams and dated 1896. I have already mentioned one type of vase made solely as presentation pieces, this is another used extensively for the same purpose. Note the crystal design – Matsu-No-Ke. 26.7 cm (10½ in) high

106   107   108   109

110   111   112   113   114

115   116   117

106 This is an American type of 'Coralene'. I have shown this specimen because although I do not have an English example in my collection I want you, the reader, to know something about this magnificent glassware. Actually Coralene is not a type, but a decoration of minute coloured beads stuck on glass of any shape or colour.

This glassware was produced on the Continent, in the U.S.A. and England in quantity around 1890. The beads were united with the glass in a number of ways. On the Continent adhesive was generally used, in the U.S.A. adhesive and muffling, but in England muffling was the 'correct' way. The tiny beads were welded on to the article. As with other countries, the colour of the articles in England ranged from crystal to all colours of the rainbow and it was the specimens of rainbow satin which were, in my opinion, the most beautiful. In the northern region a number of glass-works produced this type of glassware, but the decoration is generally on crystal and to me is not very attractive. See 439. 12.7 cm (5 in) high

107 This example is not Coralene, but the influence is there, it can be finished in the glasshouse during making, but 'true' Coralene has to be finished in another department. The canes used are 6–9 mm long, by 3 mm diameter ($\frac{1}{4}$–$\frac{3}{8}$ in by $\frac{1}{8}$ in) and were applied hot while the specimen was still plastic. The basket which is artistic rather than functional, is cased opal over pink with amber handle, feet and applied cane. Note the formation of the rim, the 3 feet, and also the colours used, all are typically Stevens & Williams. The date is a few years after Coralene, 1898. 20.3 cm (8 in) high

108 A vase made by the same firm in the same year as 107. The technique looks the same, but differs in a rather unusual way. The vase is opal, cased pink inside and outside. The extra work is to show an opal line along the top rim to match the applied cane work. Rather extravagant, but the skill was available. The rim formation is more pronounced in this example. 11.4 cm ($4\frac{1}{2}$ in) high

109 A cased opal over ruby fruit dish, so extravagantly designed and made, it can only be Boulton & Mills, Audnam. This type of design is at times the only way collectors can identify this firm's specimens, c. 1900. 25.4 cm (10 in) diameter

110 An opal jug with blue decoration. Cheap handle and weak blue colour helps to identify as Boulton & Mills, c. 1910. Only the extra weight and solid foot distinguishes it from a Continental specimen. 12.1 cm ($4\frac{3}{4}$ in) high

111 One of a pair of vases which I cannot definitely identify. Cased opal over ruby with the ruby fading as it reaches the base. It looks very much like Stevens & Williams, but the acanthus leaf is so shaped and worked, so brilliantly made, a feature I have never seen on their glass, that I think it may be Boulton & Mills, 1900. 12.7 cm (5 in) diameter

112 This is an example of the combination of 2 of Stevens & Williams's techniques, namely applied decoration and threaded ware. Being crystal it has been included only to establish the fact that crystal was used as well as colour when the firm continued the practice after 1886. Although not so plentiful as coloured, my experience has shown them very desirable. 23.5 cm ($9\frac{1}{4}$ in) high

113 An example of how opal and crystal go together when correctly designed. The usual 3 feet from the firm of Stevens & Williams, a flower prunt instead of a raspberry one is used to cover the pontil-mark, rather unusual. c. 1900. 19.1 cm ($7\frac{1}{2}$ in) high

114 A companion to the jug, 110. This type of applied work was a typical market specimen. Made by Boulton & Mills, c. 1910. 13.3 cm ($5\frac{1}{4}$ in) high

115 Although a commercial piece it is well designed and well made, cased opal over the old cherry red used by Stevens & Williams. The casings are thick and the vase heavy, the foot mould blown but is solid, rather early, around 1890. 19.1 cm ($7\frac{1}{2}$ in) high

116 An exquisite specimen by Boulton & Mills, c. 1900. Cased crystal over opal, with 3 crystal and blue acanthus leaves, finished with a large 3.8 cm ($1\frac{1}{2}$ in) diameter raspberry prunt. Simple design and extremely heavy. 33 cm (13 in) diameter

117 This example must be compared with 115 as they are both commercial and the same type. This one could be as late as 1900. The colours are very watery, the feet uneven. I cannot see why it was ever finished! It is faults of this kind the collector must get acquainted with, to achieve a first-class collection. 24.1 cm ($9\frac{1}{2}$ in) high

118

119

120

121

122

123

124

125

126

127

128

129

118 In England after 1880, an ambition or craze developed between glass-blowers to case a vase or bowl in as many colours as possible. I think 7 casings were achieved, but I have only ever seen 5. The specimen illustrated has 4, crystal over ruby over blue over crystal, which means ruby and blue are completely encased in crystal. The light blue portions have been obtained by grinding the heavy cobalt blue casing. It is signed and was made by Stevens & Williams in 1925. 22.9 cm (9 in) diameter

119 & 120 Two examples of Stevens & Williams 'Moss-Agate' – a unique type of glassware which has a number of characteristics of great interest to collectors. When once examined it cannot be confused with any other glassware of the same name. The 2 are shown together for detailed comparison.

Note the difference in shape, for the difference is startling and although this type of glassware is generally rare, I have seen many pieces, yet never 2 shapes the same – the variation seems almost intentional. Note the crizzling, a common form of decoration, but with this glassware the cracks have almost severed the vases before being sealed. In some shapes the crizzling reaches the top of the vase which is then ground flat.

Now for the mechanical decoration – the small specimen displays a cut band and I know of no other pattern being used. I have been told that engraving was tried on a few experimental pieces – but if it had been successful more examples would have been found. The cut band is the only common factor which occurs on a fair number of these vases. The coloured streaks and patches vary in density, the more colourful ones generally accompanying minute fluffy white patches which have been marvered into the glass which can be as much as 1.3 cm (½ in) thick in some places.

The colour is very important, these specimens are what the French call champagne glass, an off-white slightly clouded transparent crystal. **119:** 20.3 cm (8 in) high, **120:** 15 cm (6 in) high

121 Stevens & Williams, like Richardson's, experimented with cane work, the piece illustrated being a good example. It proved very costly to produce, and was discontinued around 1890. The top formation is typical of Stevens & Williams but the feet are lead crystal, although the usual 3 have been made in the fashion favoured by Thomas Webb. The 2 points are very important and need to be noted. 15.9 cm (6¼ in) diameter

122 This is a late example of what glassblowers in the Stourbridge area call Stevens & Williams 'Bubbly'. The first pieces were produced at least 70 years ago and were made in most colours, shapes and sizes and sometimes even cased. For the interest of the collector, the bubbles are on the inside only and in many cases they are in a regular formation having been blown in a mould. c. 1945. 26 cm (10¼ in) diameter

123 Keith Murray's renowned 'Cactus' vase – at one time very controversial, but now accepted as a work of art. Made at Stevens & Williams, c. 1934. 38.1 cm (15 in) high

124 This is a bowl made at Stevens & Williams and again designed by Keith Murray. I had seen some of the glassware designed by him at Whitefriars in the early 1930s and wondered what effect his designs would have at the Brierley Hill works. Murray's designs had a very mixed reception. Try to imagine the specimen illustrated being shown to glassmakers whose families had been making 'Victorian' glass for a hundred years. I purchased a few pieces in about 1936 knowing a change would come. Did I like them? Not his engraved crystal, but I thought the designs for his coloured ware had charm. 30.5 cm (12 in) diameter

125 An opal over ruby cased basket, made in Stourbridge by any one of the first-class firms. It is illustrated to show how well a simple design made by first-class craftsmen can compare with more richly decorated specimens. c. 1900. 17.8 cm (7 in) high

126 A little before 1870 John Northwood started to develop new styles, invent machines and techniques, in fact to revolutionize glass-making. But it was his search for new colours that interests us at this moment. The specimen shown is a decanter vase, one of many shapes which can be used as a vase. It is cased Rockingham over citron, 2 colours which figured prominently in Stevens & Williams's production until 1920. The vase is intaglio decorated not cameo (i.e., the decoration is recessed, not in relief). 31.8 cm (12½ in) high

127 This vase has only been discovered and its significance realized during the last 2 years. It is signed 'M.W. & Co. "Vitrified"' – Mills, Walker & Co., Wordsley. Little is known about this vase, but it needs to be researched. Years ago the word vitrified was used by some firms rather indiscriminately because it seemed to have sales value but G. Bacchus, Birmingham and Richardson, Stourbridge, backed their wares with skill and elegance, so much so, that every piece is desirable. The shape illustrated is rarely found in the Midlands, the glass mixture and decoration is very good, quite as good as the 2 premier firms, so if this firm had the skill to make one, there must be others. 27.9 cm (11 in) high

128 A fine example of Stevens & Williams cased Rockingham over citron over crystal known as 'Alexandrite'. The decoration is intaglio but the way it has been used makes the upper half of the vase cameo. Parts of the Rockingham colouring has been thinned to make all the casing transparent. c. 1900. 29.2 cm (11½ in) high

129 Stevens & Williams made many baskets over the years, but this specimen needs explanation. It looks like cased crystal over citron, with blue streaks and red blotches worked into the surface, then sprinkled with silver fleck, this in turn over opal. That is the obvious explanation, but after inspection I realized it had been made the other way round. The opal casing is made while the citron casing is being prepared – the colours being marvered in and the fleck included. The opal and citron casings are combined and then cracked off the blowing-iron when they are placed into the prepared crystal casing. The worker with the punty-iron has now to finish off the basket. c. 1900. 18.4 cm (7¼ in) high

130   131   132   133   134

135   136   137   138

139   140   141   142

130 Most of the glass made in Birmingham looks commercial, but some specimens made at G. Bacchus are the exception. The example shown is from their range of vitrified glass, it is signed 'Geo. Bacchus & Sons, Vitrified. Enamel Colours'. I cannot find its registration date, so it must be compared with some of the same type made by Richardson's of Stourbridge and registered in 1847.

The shapes used by the Birmingham firm are very unorthodox, compared with the classical shapes of the Stourbridge firm. Patterns, especially the monochrome, are similar, but there is a difference. The Birmingham firm used much finer transfers which gives them a true professional look. With only a little experience the two wares can easily be separated. As many of the articles of both firms are not signed, it will pay the collector to be sure, because prices vary considerably. The glass mixture of G. Bacchus is definitely better, the transfers clearer, and quantity used is less, so it is fair to assume it was made a few years later. 12.7 cm (5 in) diameter

131 Here again commercialism is very obvious with this group of wine glasses from Walsh, Walsh, Lodge Road, all are signed. They were made in at least 3 sizes, and the bowls cased with most colours over crystal. The taller goblets, about 25.4 cm (10 in) high, have the same shape and are very beautiful. To date them is difficult as they were made over a long period, 1900–38. 20.3 cm (8 in) high

132 Another example from Birmingham, signed Walsh, Walsh, England. A small bowl cased green over opal, designed for commercial production. Note the severe pattern, which automatically dates it c. 1938. With all its faults it is worth collecting if signed. 8.9 cm (3½ in) diameter

133 A much earlier specimen than 132. An ornament, because it has many uses, flower or spill holder, etc., signed Walsh, yellow iridescent, a colour very popular with this firm. These were being made from 1900. 10.2 cm (4 in) diameter

134 In 1907 John Walsh, of Birmingham, registered a new type of glassware called 'Vesta-Venetian'. It was produced in a few colours, thin and light in weight, and all pieces were iridescent. Each piece I believe was signed 'Walsh'. It is a type of glassware that must be examined before collecting for the word Venetian is so misleading. 17.1 cm (6¾ in) high

135 This is another example of Vesta-Venetian by J. Walsh, Walsh, included to show another colour. 21.6 cm (8½ in) high

136 An older vase from J. Walsh, Walsh, c. 1900, very heavy. The mixture contained uranium. As with their later wares it is iridescent. This type of vase could be found with an opalescent top and neck. 21.6 cm (8½ in) high

137 & 138 These 2 can be described together. Made at Loyd and Summerfield, Park Glass Works, Birmingham. At the Great Exhibition, 1851, the firm was congratulated on its coloured glass. In another art journal it was stated that their vases shaped like onions and leeks were original and life-like. I saw similar vases years ago, but they were always thought to be Continental, so after some examination and research I purchased a few. The 2 shapes are heavy and have been made the English way. The date, I think, would be around 1880. 137: 15.9 cm (6¼ in) high, 138: 23.5 cm (9¼ in) high

139 Around 1851, Birmingham was the centre of what can only be called a craze. Someone had an idea to fasten metal on to glass as a decoration, which meant anything from gold and silver to brass. G. Bacchus and F. & C. Osler, Broad Street, provided glass blanks and Messrs Blew & Sons, the brass castings. I believe the craze only lasted for about 10 years. 139 is a G. Bacchus crystal blank with orange and green stripes marvered into the glass and which has 2 brass castings, artificially aged, hooked on to the top of the vase, then fastened to the base ring with screws. 19.1 cm (7½ in) high

140 This example follows on from 139 but uses something quite different – pewter. 30.5 cm (12 in) high

141 This vase was made by G. Bacchus & Sons. The design is very weak, note the projecting handles – asking to be broken – and the colour combination gaudy and cheap. This type was made, I believe, to compete with Continental imports which poured into Britain before the end of the 19th century. The 3 colours were much favoured by this firm, but not often together. It was made, up to a point, the Continental way, in a mould with a large hollow foot. English glass-blowers would not make a hollow foot unless forced to do so. It could have been cracked off at the top without any further work. This the old glassmaker detested, so it was picked up on a punty-iron and the top smoothed round the English way. 29.2 cm (11½ in) high

142 A nicely balanced old fashioned vase made by G. Bacchus, cased crystal over green with pulled down top, leaving the points to be pinched the Bacchus way. Under the folds the vase has been re-heated to bring out opalescence, c. 1870. 17.8 cm (7 in) high

143   144   145   146   147

148   149   150   151

152   153   154   155

143, 145 & 146 Two vases, **143** and **145** and a bowl, **146**, have been selected to show applied surface decoration found on glassware made by James Powell & Sons (Whitefriars) London, a few years before 1920 and which continued well into the 1930s.

A ribbed band, only, on one vase, a ribbed band and tear drops on another. The bowl's outer surface has a raised pattern worked the old way called pinch-work. This type of decoration was discontinued (it was not economical) and replaced by applied threads many years later, on their 'Studio' range. All of these decorations can at times be found on one specimen in one form or another. If an article has a ribbed band and tear drops as a decoration it is 90 per cent certain to be Whitefriars.

A few words about the ribbed band. At first glance it can be mistaken for a similar band found on Stevens & Williams's 'Moss-Agate'. The difference is very easy to detect. Whitefriars' band is ribbed or decorated during the blowing with a knurling tool, a rotating wheel about 2.5 cm (1 in) diameter with various patterns on the diameter face. The Stevens & Williams band is cut after the vase is finished and cold.

A vase similar to **145** with different coloured tears can be seen at the Victoria & Albert Museum, London. It is the work of that fine glassmaker from Whitefriars, the late Tom Hill.

To help the collector, certain innovations which occurred during the production of this glassware, can be explained. Firstly, we find engraving being added for decoration, a type of blanket engraving which was used a great deal in the 18th century, patterns without detail. Another addition was the use of gold-leaf in the stems and knops of goblets, all very Venetian. A few months ago I examined some of these specimens at Whitefriars and I had to be convinced that they had not been made in Venice. **143**: 14 cm (5½ in) high, **145**: 16.5 cm (6½ in) high, **146**: 24.1 cm (9½ in) diameter

144 A paperweight made at Whitefriars by Tom Hill, in 1954, to show how coloured canes alter when re-heated. The original canes were red, white and blue. 7.6 cm (3 in) diameter

147 This type of perfume bottle is so controversial, I would like to add my experience. They are invariably sold as Stourbridge ink bottles. I have lived in the Stourbridge area for 70 years, and 50 of those have been spent seeking for and talking glass, visiting families and works. I have even carried this specimen about with me, and nowhere have I found any evidence of anyone knowing anyone who made it or know if they were made locally. A few millefiore perfume bottles were made, most being friggers, although nothing like the one illustrated. But we must also bear in mind that there are hundreds all over England, so whoever made them was certainly in production for some time.

I have not yet inquired at Whitefriars, but *my* view is that they began to make them about 1880 and continued intermittently until closing down in 1980. 15.2 cm (6 in) high

148–151 Four specimens of glassware made at Battersea, London, 1925–35, every piece being signed 'Gray-Stan'. It will be very difficult to find a pair of any type because very few specimens were duplicated, although they do exist. Goblets were an exception, as they were made in sets.

During my visits to London, I was told that each glass-blower designed his own creation, which seems unbelievable. Nevertheless very few pairs are found, and the works were only in production for about 10 years. These 4 do seem to lack design development, but occasionally we come across an exceptional piece, see **153**. **148**: 18.4 cm (7¼ in) high, **149**: 26.7 cm (10½ in) high, **150**: 23.5 cm (9¼ in) high, **151**: 21.6 cm (8½ in) high

152 This is from a series of machine-pressed vases, the mould being made for J. Jenkins & Sons Ltd., China and Glass Merchants, London, in 1935. This specimen was made in Czechoslovakia and depicts the last of the Revenge, signed Barolac (see page 33.) 20.3 cm (8 in) high

153 This is an example of 'Gray-Stan' totally different in style, in fact so different, it needed the signature to convince me. The maker was without doubt an Italian. The glass mixture, which is lead crystal, forced him to increase the various thicknesses which in turn added to the weight. The foot is typically Venetian in shape. Note how the foot edge is turned up and over, and also the dolphin stem, a style used in Venice. Next the dish, by no means an English shape, the early Nailsea pattern was used on the Continent. But it is a very beautiful specimen and could settle many arguments. 22.9 cm (9 in) high

154 Another example of 'Gray-Stan'. Notice the similarity to **149**, **150** and **151**. 26.7 cm (10½ in) high

155 A specimen made at Bermondsey Glass Works, London, c. 1900. The pressed head is signed Guy Underwood, and registered 'Applied Art', London. Another example, **322**, from the same works emphasizes the diversity of styles produced. 17.2 cm (6¾ in) high

156 157 158 159 160 161

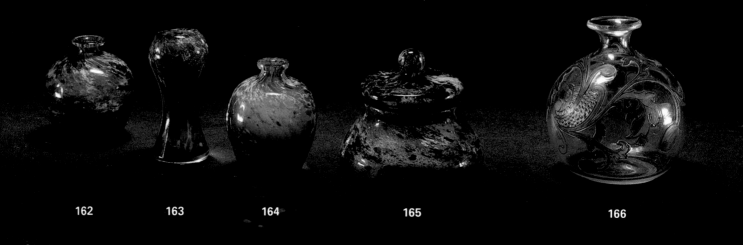

162 163 164 165 166

167 168 169 170 171

156 & 157 A number of coloured specimens made at Webb–Corbett, Coalbournhill Glass Works, Stourbridge, are shown on this page. None of them is an art treasure, but are first-class commercial pieces and very worthy of collection.

The collector will require a great deal of experience to identify them, as very few were signed. By consulting the illustrations some of their characteristics can be indicated but I am afraid not very effectively. The first specimens, an enamelled tumbler and jug, are recognized by their decoration as they are the work of Hugo Maisey, a Bohemian artist who came to Stourbridge in 1912. He restricted himself to certain colours, which is a great help to collectors, and he favoured designs with subjects such as cascades or bands of small flowers and leaves with a matt finish. Two very important pointers to his work are the matt coloured surface and his shade of green. **156:** 6.6 cm ($2\frac{5}{8}$ in) high, **157:** 17.2 cm ($6\frac{3}{4}$ in) high

158 This small jug is a splendid example of Hugo Maisey's work. The colour, surface and designs explain his style perfectly. 10.8 cm ($4\frac{1}{4}$ in) diameter

159 The work on this jug by the same artist has the largest surface area I have known him to decorate, so, coupled with the fact that I am sure Webb–Corbett did not make the jug, the date is later than the previous examples of his work which were before 1914. The jug appears to be one made by Boulton & Mills, which closed down before 1926. Hugo Maisey died in 1932, so the date is after 1919 and not later than 1932. 20.3 cm (8 in) high

160 Another example of a Webb–Corbett vase decorated by Hugo Maisey. Note the professionalism, a few lines, a small splash of colour and a picture lives, all in a few minutes, c. 1920. 20.3 cm (8 in) high

161 A Webb–Corbett goblet decorated by Hugo Maisey, a slightly different design, well covered but not embarrassingly so, c. 1914. 15.9 cm ($6\frac{1}{4}$ in) high

162–165 Four examples of cased splash glassware exclusively Webb–Corbett, about 1920. A crystal blank is splashed and marvered in with the colours illustrated, and finally cased with crystal. **162, 163** and **164** are a set of 3 vases, the centre one is signed Webb & Corbett, England, **165** is a covered bowl made in the same glassware. **162 & 164:** 12.1 cm ($4\frac{3}{4}$ in) high, **163:** 13.7 cm ($5\frac{3}{8}$ in) high, **165:** 15.2 cm (6 in) diameter

166 During the cameo period many Midland glassworks tried to imitate cameo in a cheaper form. The example shown was made by Webb–Corbett in their original factory, The White House Glass Works, Wordsley, about 1900 and signed Thomas Webb & Corbett Ltd., Stourbridge, England. It is a well-designed and manufactured piece and should be collected as 'pseudo-cameo'. It was blown in a mould, polished and enamelled. 15.2 cm (6 in) diameter

167 This wine glass was made at one of the earliest recorded glassworks in the Stourbridge area, namely The Heath Glassworks which were demolished before 1900. They were made in at least 3 sizes, crystal and ruby over crystal, often accompanied by a decanter. They look very Continental, and many dealers refuse to accept them as English. Nevertheless they are Stourbridge made. 10.2 cm (4 in) high

168 Ornamental wines were very common in England in Victorian times, ornamental being the operative word, because they were quite useless for the task. This example was made at Bromsgrove and was of a type regularly sold in my local markets as late as 1920. 15.2 cm (6 in) high

169, 170 & 171 Three of the oldest cased specimens I have been able to find in the Midlands. They were made at S. Edwards, Gladstone Road, Collaston, Stourbridge. Records go back to 1880 but are incomplete. S. Edwards traded as a professional glassmaker, Novelty Glass Works, all very quaint. My research points to a little after 1850! All the casings are weak and patchy. On **169** the opal is thin and patchy, the enamelled design and colours very early Victorian. **170** and **171** have many manufacturing faults. Surprisingly they are 3-cased, crystal over pink over opal. The crystal was much too cold when being used, showing tool marks and heavy pressure in many places. The pontils show a small gathering of bottle glass. These shapes and colours have long ago disappeared from this area. **169:** 17.1 cm ($6\frac{3}{4}$ in) high, **170:** 20.3 cm (8 in) high, **171:** 21.6 cm ($8\frac{1}{2}$ in) high

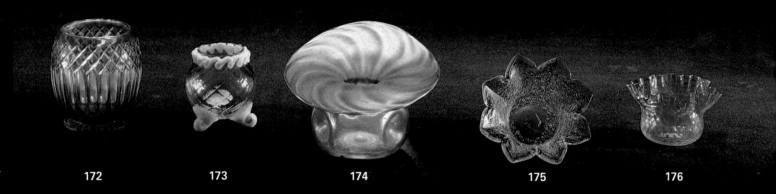

172   173   174   175   176

177   178   179   180   181   182

183   184   185

172 I have included this specimen of cased glass over citron made by Thomas Webb because of its likeness to Stevens & Williams's 'Alexandrite'. Although Alexandrite's outer case is Rockingham (chocolate) when applied as a thin case it is identical to this example. Another guide for the collector is that I have never seen any decoration other than cutting used on Thomas Webb's ware. c. 1925. 10.2 cm (4 in) high

173 Not an art piece by any means but everything about it is Thomas Webb: the mould pattern, the form of pinch-work around the top, the claw-feet and the off-white opal. I expect it was made in many colours and other sizes. c. 1924. 7.6 cm (3 in) high

174 The interest in iridescent glassware started when ancient glass vessels were found which had been buried for centuries and glassmakers tried to imitate the iridescent surface. This continued for more than a hundred years, but it was around 1870 when it became a craze.

Glassmakers say the iridescence is either on the glass, or in it: the collector, if he has the opportunity, should lightly rub an obscure part of the article – if the iridescence begins to fade, let alone come away, it is surface applied only. Theoretically, the value then is much lower, unless the piece has a signature or trademark. Two outstanding trademarks are Louis Comfort Tiffany (L.C.T.) or any associated with Frederick Carder. Pieces with an English trademark are generally very good because the oxides which are sprayed on, are applied when the articles are being made and still at working temperature. The iridescence arrived at in this way, if not permanent, is satisfactory, the perfect way is to case the oxidation with crystal. The date I think would be after Webb's Bronze of 1878, but before 1900. Webb's Iris. 15.9 cm (6¼ in) diameter

175 A small bowl which at first seems insignificant but it is the shape of the top which I want collectors to note. I have seen it used on vases and illustrated in Thomas Webb's records of 1889. The example shown has 10 points, but I have seen it with 6 and 8 points. For identification purposes it is almost a Webb's trademark, used in many colours and on most types of glassware. The specks seen in the illustration

are pieces of crushed crystal, marvered in the blank during the making. 12.7 cm (5 in) diameter

176 This example is a rare piece of Thomas Webb's 'Alexandrite' first made in 1901. The size and shape is used in many types of their glassware, but only in the colours shown is it valuable. The original colour is pale citron, the pink and blue shading to purple is a re-heated part, so the re-coloured areas can vary greatly as can the shape, for some pieces have feet, others flared tops. A common factor is the thin metal. 10.2 cm (4 in) diameter

177 & 178 Practically every glassworks in all the regions of England had, and still have, their 'bread and butter' lines. It could be lampshades (incidentally shades for oil, gas or electricity were the principal articles of production for scores of glassworks from 1900–25), epergnes, salt cellars, sugar and creams, etc. The firms in the Stourbridge area made all of these, with each firm specializing and with care we can identify each pair, since each bears some small feature of the firm worked into them. The sugar and cream illustrated were made at Thomas Webb's about 1930. The bowl and cream jug are mould blown, with the firm's 'Moire' pattern. The sugar is 15.2 cm (6 in) high

179 This is an example of Webb's iridescent. It followed the successful production of their 'Bronze' in 1878. There are a number of shapes which differ only in the length of the neck and colour of the claw decoration. The claw I have seen in opal, green and ruby. This claw, and others found on Webb's specimens, should be memorized – as they are mould-made they can almost be treated as a trademark. 15.2 cm (6 in) high

180 This is an example of Thomas Webb's very successful 'Sunshine Amber' (not to be confused with their 'Sunset' which is decorated with their fir cone pattern). The shades of this glassware vary considerably, so much so, that it is possible there were a number of different mixtures. It is moulded with their wave pattern. 25.4 cm (10 in) high

181 This is an example of what old glassmakers called Webb's 'Honey', but I have seen this colour made into a vase exactly the size and shape of 180. Could 'Sunshine Amber' cover a range of amber shades? 15.9 cm (6¼ in) high

182 Around 1900 Thomas Webb made at least 2 types of ashtrays similar in shape to the one illustrated. The other specimen had flowers instead of leaves, both were green. Note the shape of the foot for identification purposes. 21 cm (8¼ in) high

183 Blowing and shaping a large gathering of glass has never been popular with English glass-blowers, but with the added chore of colour over opal, moulding the diamond air traps and finally casing with crystal, the reader can appreciate that specimens of rainbow satin like this are not plentiful. The makers of this piece I believe to be Thomas Webb, the date around 1890. There are a number of imperfections, such as stones in the metal, the air traps slightly out of control and just a little off perpendicular. But even with these faults, a piece of this type cannot be refused. 33 cm (13 in) high

184 In 1900 2 Stourbridge area glassworks, Thomas Webb and Stevens & Williams, produced a rather unusual type of glass called 'Trellisware'. The example illustrated was made at Thomas Webb's. At first I thought it purely decorative, but later I found that there should be a ruby liner, so that it could be used to hold flowers. Those made at Stevens & Williams were period pieces in goblet form, the stems and feet were normal, but the bowl was replaced by trellis work, and would seem to be for decoration only. 30.5 cm (12 in) high

185 A vase for identification, most deceptive. The first impression is obviously French, but Thomas Webb's records (sketch-book of 1879) describe them as alabaster-cored, with square top and enamelled, and it is only when a number are placed alongside each other that this is realized, all differ in some way. 19.7 cm (7¾ in) high

186

187

188

189

190

191

192

193

194

195

196

197

198

186 This is a specimen of applied work which I find very difficult to fault. The gold ruby used to make the basket is of exceptional brilliance even for a Stourbridge firm. Designing a basket of this type needed a worker with a complete knowledge of the glasshouse, and a gaffer and servitor who understood each other perfectly. It has a touch of commercialism which guarantees a sale, and could have been made at a number of glasshouses in the area, but my guess is Thomas Webb around 1900. 21.6 cm (8½ in) high

187 Another piece with applied crystal decoration and an ideal specimen for collectors. It is a little unusual to get so many of a firm's characteristics on one article. A rich ruby bowl, feet made with the help of a specially designed mould, the style of chain work, and the massive raspberry prunts, all combined with a little commercialism. Thomas Webb, c. 1900. 16.5 cm (6½ in) diameter

188 A cased bowl ruby over white, with applied crystal pinch-work. The contrast in shades is obtained by using a pillar mould, and twisting when withdrawing. The lavish use of crystal pinch-work is noticeable on Thomas Webb's early specimens, c. 1900. 15.2 cm (6 in) diameter

189 & 190 A ruby sugar and cream by Thomas Webb, c. 1900. The shape of the feet is again apparent. 15.2 cm (6 in) diameter of basin

191 The colour, which is the predominent feature of this jug, seemed to lose popularity in Stourbridge some years before 1900. It is nicely designed and well made. A calculated guess indicates Thomas Webb, for the diamond pattern is almost certain to be from their mould. 22.9 cm (9 in) high

192 Particular notice should be taken of the colour of this bowl. It is cased crystal over tinted opal and the splashes were intended to imitate millefiore canes. They were first made as lampshades, with a rim instead of a base, but developed as illustrated. The bowls are rare and the splashes identify the firm – Thomas Webb. Production of shades and bowls covered the years 1900–30. 27.3 cm (10¾ in) diameter

193 A fine example of acid-etched crystal cameo. Although this is a crystal example, specimens in self-colours and occasionally rainbow were made, chiefly by Richardson's. The authentic pieces are very expensive, so a warning to the budding collector. During the acid-etching period 1870–1914, machine-pressed articles of a similar type were produced chiefly in the north of England, so it is wise to seek advice before purchasing. The pattern on this example stands proud by 0.8 mm ($\frac{1}{32}$ in), but, 1.6 mm ($\frac{1}{16}$ in) is not uncommon. 27.9 cm (11 in) across

194 A matt or satin finished ruby posy bowl with applied crystal leaves. To find applied articles completely matt is unusual. Why? I cannot tell, because it only takes a very short time to give them an acid dip. Any one of the Midlands' firms could have produced this example. 14 cm (5½ in) diameter

195 As already stated, most firms made variations of pseudo-cameo. This amethyst example made at Thomas Webb's is mould blown and very heavy. There may be other colours, but I know the decoration was left as it came from the mould or simply cleaned up around the edges with an engraving wheel. c. 1910. 14 cm (5½ in) high

196 An unsigned 3-cased cameo vase, white over ruby over yellow. As it is unsigned we can only guess the artist, but there is little doubt that J. T. Fereday was that person. As this book was designed not to accept glassware out of reach of the average collector, cameo must be kept to a minimum, so an example, unsigned, but with characteristics which almost prove its provenance, was chosen. First of all Fereday's favourite colours were yellow, white and red, then notice the neck pattern, variations of which he worked on. He liked to see a butterfly in the design, and there is a large one on the reverse side. The frontal design is a well-known Thomas Webb pattern. I suggest it was made before 1911, because his friend George Woodall was still at Thomas Webb, and it is always understood they worked well together. 19.1 cm (7½ in) high

197 Another example of Webb pseudo-cameo. It was made in at least 4 colours with stippled and frosted backgrounds. I have seen many shapes and sizes, but they all resemble the one shown. Production of these continued until 1936. 22.2 cm (8¾ in) high

198 A ruby and pale yellow striped vase, elaborately decorated with crystal pinch-work. Note again the feet formation. Many of this style have an additional raspberry prunt on the pontil mark. Thomas Webb 1900. 10.8 cm (4½ in) high

199   200   201   202   203

204   205   206   207   208

209   210   211   212   213

A full page of opalescent glassware will not discredit any book devoted to coloured Victorian glass. It has been known and appreciated for hundreds of years in every glass area in the world, but no more than in the English Midlands, Stourbridge in particular. Very little skill is required to get the effect, but very careful planning is needed to produce first-class art pieces. More details on page 33.

199 Very pleasing to the eye, this example of opalescence has needed a fair amount of skill to transfer the flats of the 8-sided trumpet right down to the knop, where it joins the foot. This was no problem for Thomas Webb who produced fine specimens in this type of glassware. The glass mixture is a little disappointing, for it lacks that extra uranium touch (yellow). Before 1914. 41.3 cm ($16\frac{1}{4}$ in) high

200 An example of how a raised pattern can enhance opalescent glass. Made at Thomas Webb, but needs more uranium. When glass made with a prepared mixture is re-heated we get an opalescent effect, so in simple terms a raised pattern gently re-heated turns white. With a threaded foot and a few raspberry prunts, we get an above-the-average specimen. 1900–10. 29.8 cm ($11\frac{3}{4}$ in) high

201 A discrete application of colour in the form of green indentation balancing what otherwise would have been a rather dreary specimen. This vase, I feel, would be better with additional uranium. Obviously the same firm about the same date. 26.7 cm ($10\frac{1}{2}$ in) high

202 This vase was made at one of 2 glassworks, Thomas Webb or Richardson's, Wordsley. I believe Richardson's. The design on the vase is their well-known horse-chestnut leaf pattern. The firm's glasshouse closed about 1926 and Thomas Webb purchased the leaf pattern mould in about 1936 and used it, so we can find similar vases made by the 2 firms. To the dedicated collector I suggest one reasonably sure way of distinguishing specimens. That is by the amount of uranium in the glass mixture. Most glassworks used this at various times in some of their glassware, but Thomas Webb used more than most. They knew they could not improve the article, only the colour, and by adding extra uranium they could certainly do that. Should the collector

come across any kind of article with this pattern and the colour of a lemon, it will have been made by Thomas Webb. 22.2 cm ($8\frac{3}{4}$ in) high

203 A totally different type of opalescent. Everything suggests Stevens & Williams as the manufacturers. Size, weight (1.6 kg, $3\frac{1}{2}$ lb) and above all their use of pillar moulds, are their features, correct for this type of vase. c. 1910. 46.3 cm ($18\frac{1}{4}$ in) high

204–207 These 4 can be discussed together as they are part of a table decoration, see page 34. They were made at Thomas Webb's, c. 1900. **204**: 10.2 cm (4 in) high, **205**: 20.3 cm (8 in) high, **206**: 25.4 cm (10 in) high, **207**: 35.6 cm (14 in) high

208 Another item of table decoration used in a similar way as the 4 previous pieces, but more decorative. The centre-piece would be very impressive. Made by Thomas Webb about 1900. Discussed with previous other pieces on page 34. 22.9 cm (9 in) high

209 This comes under opalescent, but has a number of innovations. The underside of the tray has pattern acid-etched, of a style described for **193**, with a stem like **199**. The foot is generally reserved for first-class articles. Skill is written all over it, but I think it is 'gilding the lily'! Made by Thomas Webb, c. 1910. 13.3 cm ($5\frac{1}{4}$ in) diameter

210 A very extravagant piece. Again the opalescence takes second place. It is used only for the top edge to give shape. The dish itself is blown in a diamond patterned mould, and has Webb's claw feet with a prunt over the pontil-mark. Pinch-work was used extensively by this firm, but do not rely on it too much, as other glassworks used it, too. 17.2 cm ($6\frac{3}{4}$ in) diameter

211 An opalescent example made by Richardson's. Note the small amount of uranium used. Particular notice should be taken of the turn-over top, (see page 34). The shape of the foot was common practice throughout the Midlands. c. 1900. 10.8 cm ($4\frac{1}{4}$ in) diameter

212 There are hundreds of specimens very much like this example, in many shops and most are foreign. It is extremely difficult to separate them. Experience is needed as they have been copied all over the world. There are very few definite ways of telling them apart, but my comments may help. Always suspect a gaudy coloured specimen. English types are generally shades rather than colours. The feet on English specimens are sometimes lead crystal, but never on foreign ones. Notice how smooth the English pieces are when finished. Every part seems to have been made, not just stuck together. Dates are just guesswork. 19.1 cm ($7\frac{1}{2}$ in) high

213 This example looks very neat and elegant. It is, but very commercial, nicely designed for production. Thomas Webb possibly between the wars. 21 cm ($8\frac{1}{4}$ in) high

214 215 216 217 218

219 220 221 222 223 224

225 226 227 228

By now the reader must have realized the overwhelming number of opalescent specimens made by Thomas Webb, between 1890 and 1910. Not until I began to collect and research this type of glassware did I realize this fact. Thousands of articles were made in cribs, chiefly because it could be decorated in this manner without additional expense, but very few pieces are worth collecting. Webb's pieces always seem to be designed both for shape and colour, unlike a lot of crib work where it was left to the glasshouse to decide.

214 This is a moulded dish of Webb's Lemonscent ware. Notice how effective this glassware is when projections are included in the design, c. 1910. 14 cm ($5\frac{1}{2}$ in) diameter

215 An example of blue opalescent. I understand that blue is a very difficult colour to manipulate, so it will be more difficult to discover such specimens. A description I feel sure is not needed, the illustration says it all. Thomas Webb, 1910. 13.3 cm ($5\frac{1}{4}$ in) high

216 Another piece made by Thomas Webb. Note the top formation together with the smoothly applied chain work. In this case ruby and opalescent are separated, c. 1900. 14.6 cm ($5\frac{3}{4}$ in) high

217 An example of ruby opalescent. Compare this specimen with **220**. It is an example of excellent crib work, but it is good enough to have come from a Birmingham glassworks. The style, although not necessarily the design, is rustic and Victorian. Years ago it was loosely called 'fairground stuff', but this specimen, although it looks cheap, has been made in a more sophisticated manner. The body is cased crystal over ruby, unusual for a crib job. This fact alone puts its manufacture into a glassworks better equipped than the average crib. The shape, having curves in 3 directions, always caused trouble pairing them up at the end of a shift. It could be as early as 1890, and certainly looks more old-fashioned than the streamlined **220**. 16.5 cm ($6\frac{1}{2}$ in) high

218 Another flower vase from the north, small but exquisite. Colour rich, body press-moulded with a pattern, which has been well thought out to receive opalescence. Even the pontil-mark has been threaded c. 1910. 10.2 cm (4 in) high

219 A very unusual pressed bowl from Thomas Webb. Not a very imposing specimen leaving much to be desired. The mould pattern is blurred but it looks like a Richardson mould. If it is, the date would be c. 1936. 15.2 cm (6 in) diameter

220 An opalescent ruby vase, illustrated to show 2 questionable features. The top is completely out of character with English glassware and must always be viewed with suspicion as far as identification is concerned. This type of deeply flared top is against the principle of glassworkers, who think it cheapens their work. At first glance the feet look Continental, but if examined it will be seen that the pontil is on the foot pad itself which is the English way to work. In other words the gathering of crystal is applied to the partly blown vase, then passed on to the punty-iron. The vase and foot are then finished together in one operation on the punty-iron. The Continental way is reversed, which shows the pontil between the vase and foot. The top flares have been thickened considerably. I believe this vase was made at Birmingham about 1890. 17.8 cm (7 in) high

221 Another product from Thomas Webb, crystal over ruby opalescent vase. Note the corrugated top in reverse. The folded top is for the vase to be used on a narrow shelf. c. 1900. 22.2 cm ($8\frac{3}{4}$ in) high

222 This vase has been carried almost to the limit of development. The walls of the vase are 6 mm ($\frac{1}{4}$ in) thick, and moulded with Webb's well-known 'Cascade' pattern. It has been cased ruby, only a short distance from the top, which has been squared, French fashion. After all this, it was re-heated to opalescent. The mixture, having its fair share of uranium, coupled with the deep cascade pattern, has made a magnificent specimen. c. 1910. 21 cm ($8\frac{1}{4}$ in) high

223 This opalescent vase was made a little before 1900 at Stevens & Williams. The decoration includes threads, for which they were famous. Notice that a minimum amount of uranium is used. 16.5 cm ($6\frac{1}{2}$ in) high

224 Note the likeness to **211**. Made at Richardson's about the same time, 1900. See how the green (a favourite colour at the works) resists opalescent. The top is reversed but still well finished. 14 cm ($5\frac{1}{2}$ in) diameter

225 A special piece of Richardson's moulded ruby opalescent. Observe the pattern, originally exclusively theirs, but I believe sold to Thomas Webb in 1936. This is not a tea pot! It was used to fill containers for oil lamps, with paraffin, c. 1890–1920. 16.5 cm ($6\frac{1}{2}$ in) high

226 Just one of the thousands of opalescent bells produced in England 1860–1920. Made at Stourbridge but almost impossible to state which factory, as moulds for bells like this one, were loaned to other firms. Made in pairs and sets of 3, the latter number being most desirable. 29.2 cm ($11\frac{1}{2}$ in) high

227 Lampshades were 'bread and butter' lines for hundreds of glassworks throughout Britain. They followed fairly regular shapes, but varied tremendously in colours and sizes. At times, shades for oil, gas, and electric lights were being produced simultaneously around 1910. A specimen like this is an early oil shade and many used to 'fly' during manufacture. If the crack held, it would be passed through. This was made as late as 1920 at Bolton Bowater, Platts, Amblecote. 14 cm ($5\frac{1}{2}$ in) lamp-fitting size

228 Just an ornament, rare because easily broken. I believe this pump was made at Walsh, Walsh, Birmingham about 1900. They were making various specimens of 'Rusticana' at this time. The Stourbridge type looked more like a pump, and unbroken ones are rare. 24.1 cm ($9\frac{1}{2}$ in) high

229

230

231

232

233

234

235

236

237

238

239

240

The introduction of 'Monart Ware' made at John Moncrieff Ltd., Perth, Scotland, as Victorian glass may raise a few eyebrows. It was last made c. 1960, well outside the Victorian period, but it was much the same as that made in 1924 which is well within my period. Personally, I feel justified in including it for another reason. This type of glassware was being experimented with as early as 1915 in France, and as far as I can ascertain, when introduced in Scotland in 1924 it was the first time the manufacturing technique had been commercialized.

When Salvador Ysart perfected 'Monart' it was sold only as flower-holders, but I noticed that 2 distinct styles had developed. One, a type of vase with fairly regular shapes, in every colour imaginable, and I quote from one of their catalogues. 'There is no type of flower that has not here its ideal receptacle.' Secondly, art specimens which had controlled patterns worked into the glass, and a surface decoration which in some cases represented coloured foreign timbers.

There is one controversial issue which surfaces time and time again – was Monart ever signed? The official reply is 'Only with a one inch diameter disc on which are the words "Moncrieff Scotland Monart Glass".' I raised this question with the then Works Secretary who stated it was the work's policy never to sign any piece. I questioned some of the glassmakers who said that if any were signed, it would be after the glass had left the works. The word Monart is a combination of Moncrieff and Ysart. The following 8 examples range in date from 1924 to 1939.

229 A Monart art piece with coloured enamels mixed with gold fleck worked into the bowl. The point to note is that the enamels are under control. 25.4 cm (10 in) diameter

230 Like **229**, scrolls are much in evidence, but with this example the enamels are worked on the surface and stand proud of it. 22.9 cm (9 in) high

231 Another example of the enamels being worked into glass. Although this bowl may look more attractive than **229** because of its delicate colouring, the reader should not be deceived, as the glass in **229** is very much thicker and more exacting to work. 25.4 cm (10 in) diameter

232 A cased vase made in the same manner as **236** but crystal over a special colour to look like mahogany. It may not be everyone's idea of that kind of wood, but it's a good attempt in my opinion. 23.4 cm (9 in) high

233 I fancy this specimen of Monart was made more quickly than any of the previous pieces. In fact it appears to have been started in a mould. The enamel lines would, in the first place have been vertical, and twisted when being withdrawn from the mould. 18.4 cm (7¼ in) high

234 Another cased specimen, mottled casing over white. The manufacturing technique is the same for **235**. When a cased vase is first blown, it is very much smaller than the finished size, so before the final shaping, the outer case only is deeply marked with a piece of sharp metal (a nail will do) after which the blowing is continued, and the outside casing breaks at the marks. 17.8 cm (7 in) high

235 An example of 3-cased Monart, brown over white over coral. I always thought that cased Monart would have been towards the end of its manufacture, but some years ago Mr. P. Ysart, Junior, assured me that cased pieces were some of the earliest made. 25.4 cm (10 in) high

236 A cased example, crystal over white, but with a different decorating technique. When the white blank is partly blown, a pattern is enamelled over it. The crystal casing follows, sealing the pattern on the white casing. The vase is then finally blown and finished. 22.9 cm (9 in) high

237 An example of 'Vasart' made by Salvador Ysart, the same glassman who had introduced 'Monart' in 1924. The manufacture of Monart had ceased during the war years 1939–45, so in 1945 Mr. Ysart and 2 of his sons started a small glassworks by the River Tay in Perth making 'Vasart' a similar glassware to 'Monart', signing most with a rough wheel, 'Vasart'. After their departure, I asked John Moncrieff for a few special pieces of Monart, and was told they were unable to obtain a supply of the correct coloured glass rods as they came from East Germany. I have often wondered if Salvador Ysart had the same trouble with 'Vasart', for generally it lacks Monart's brightness. 21 cm (8¼ in) diameter

238 An example of signed 'Clutha', made by James Couper & Son, City Glass Works, Glasgow, 1850–1921. For those collecting 'Clutha' I suggest they research it thoroughly before buying. Although James Couper operated from 1850 to 1921, I can only find specimens made between 1885–1900 which are of interest to collectors.

I believe there are only 2 reasons why it is bought at all. The first is that Queen Victoria admired it when she visited the factory, and second, that the firm employed 2 first-class designers, namely Christopher Dresser and George Walton. To find signed pieces is almost impossible but unsigned are to be found. See page 34. 23.5 cm (9¼ in) high

239 An unsigned example of 'Clutha'. 9.5 cm (3¾ in) diameter

240 An unusual specimen which was sold to me 25 years ago as blue 'Clutha' long before any interest was shown in this type of glassware. 8.9 cm (3½ in) high

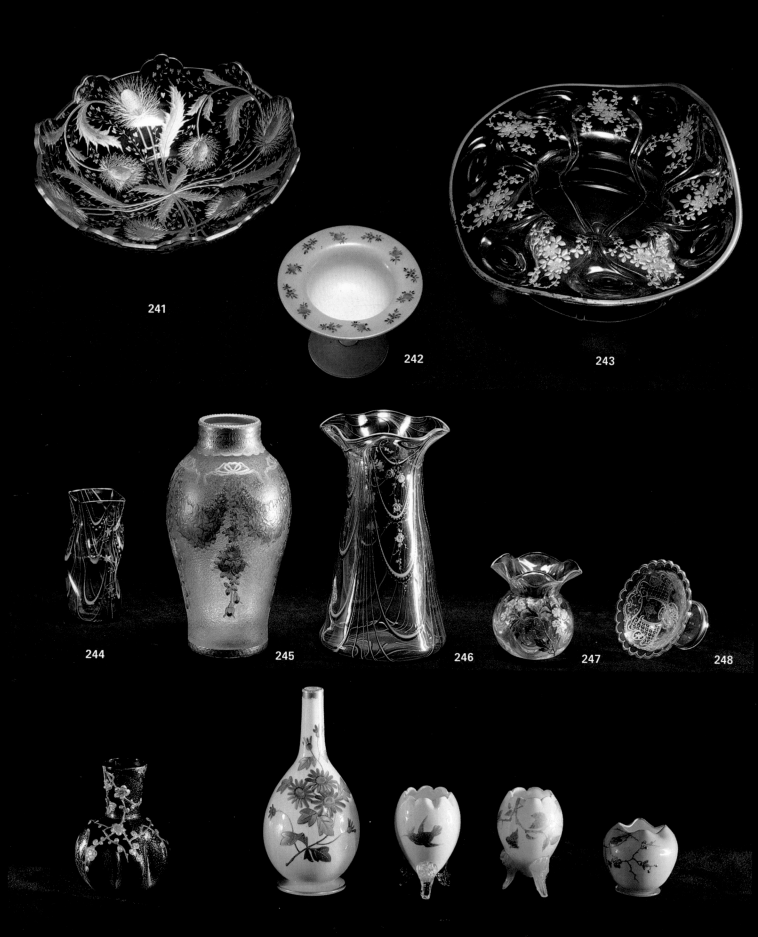

241

242

243

244   245   246   247   248

249   250   251   252   253

The 8 pieces **241–248** are all examples of gilding and enamelling decoration completed by Jules Barbe. The articles are mostly crystal with engraving on the underside which is filled, or partly filled, with gold. Jules Barbe worked at Thomas Webb for 20 years, 1880–1900, during which time he signed very few pieces. It was between 1900 and 1925 when he was working on his own that he signed most of his work. He had few assistants, one of note was Will Capewell who produced some fine work for Stevens & Williams.

241 This illustrates a type of gilding which was very common on the Continent. When produced by English firms the specimens can generally be accepted as first class and this one made by Thomas Webb, c. 1890, is no exception. 23.5 cm (9¼ in) diameter

242 This is a Burmese wine with the top folded back for Jules Barbe to decorate and this he did with red roses, but as Burmese turns red on re-heating the exercise was a failure. However good an artist is, he can make mistakes. c. 1910. 11.4 cm (4½ in) diameter

243 This is one of a series of soda-lime bowls and vases produced in 1900 with 'Cairngoram drops with green centres on flint'. This is from Thomas Webb's records, and it's their spelling. The bowl was gilded by Jules Barbe and across the polished pontil is written 'July 11th 1907', but the space allocated for his signature is left vacant. The bowl was actually decorated for a friend of mine, but never signed. 26 cm (10¼ in) diameter

244 One of Thomas Webb's soda-lime series and there is only a small amount of Jules Barbe's work, but it does show how far Stourbridge developed the Nailsea pattern. Exclude the gilding and blue spots, and look only at the worked-in pattern. This is exactly how Manchester and Northern glassworkers produced their Nailsea patterns, 1900–10. What has been done here is extremely rare for a Midland glassworks. 14 cm (5½ in) high

245 To try to judge this vase by any means other than a personal examination is futile, for each rose has had individual attention. Even the gilding has to be examined with a magnifying glass to see the true detailed work. This is Jules Barbe at his best, and is one of a pair, both signed J. BARBE. The design I think was inspired by Thomas Webb's cascade pattern and the date before 1914. 26 cm (10¼ in) high

246 This is another example of Thomas Webb's soda-lime series. The decoration is typical of Jules Barbe's work although the vase is more orthodox and taller than he generally worked on. The Nailsea pattern is very similar to **244**. c. 1900–10. 25.4 cm (10 in) high

247 These flower bowls were made in many sizes and are included in Thomas Webb's soda-lime series. For many years I have seen them in antique shops priced very low, although I admit that they are commercial. Many collectors think they are foreign, they are not! c. 1910. 10.8 cm (4¼ in) high

248 This small bowl, (and I have only seen it in one size) was made in fair numbers and was a commercial issue. Two people decorated them, namely Jules Barbe, and Will Capewell who told me how he used to tease Jules Barbe by telling him that he, Will Capewell, could decorate them as well and much faster than the master! c. 1900–6. 11.4 cm (4½ in) diameter

The following 5 examples are signed with what I call an adopted trademark, because at the present moment there is nothing official to prove it is a registered mark. A drawing of it is shown in the trademark section on page 116. During the last few years it has been more or less accepted as the trademark of Edward Webb, Whitehouse Glass Works, Wordsley, 1851–72. This may be true, but since he had the factory for only 20 years and the styles of glassware cover more years than that, I wonder if there is some other explanation. In 1850 one of the Ensell family of glassmakers had a business in Stourbridge as a dealer in all kinds of glassware. Could it be that he bought this glass from one of the local works and had his trademark painted on? All of the marks are hand painted; in no way are they commercial.

249 This is perplexing to say the least, the gilding, silver fleck, and wear marks on the base, all point to its manufacture between 1851–72. The ground and polished pontil is one of the best I have ever seen, it seems as if the makers knew that a trademark was to be applied. 14.6 cm (5¾ in) high

250 The decoration on this example is very crude but the pontil has been nicely finished, perhaps for the same reason as **249**. The shape is very old, but there is little wear on the base, and neither is there on its fellow, as it is one of a pair. 22.2 cm (8¾ in) high

251 & 252 These 2, I firmly believe, were made at Stevens & Williams, much later than 1872. This opal mixture and shaped body were used with various feet formations. The gilding is totally different, the pattern being engraved before gilding. If my judgment is correct the date would be around 1890. Both 11.4 cm (4½ in) high

253 This is cased pink over white, and is an old and cheap specimen. I have seen and examined scores of specimens with this trademark. Some are worthy of any museum, others are only cullet. Why should any firm sign such a poor piece? 8.9 cm (3½ in) diameter

254   255   256   257   258   259

260   261   262   263   264

265   266   267   268   269   270   271

254 A well-balanced shape with a single rich colour, always Richardson's main objective. c. 1900. 19.1 cm (7½ in) high

255 A Flakestone vase which could have been made, c. 1920, either by Richardson's or Thomas Webb. Both firms used the same manufacturing methods but varied the colours. The casings go as follows: a blue blank is blown; very thin pieces of coloured glass are marvered into it, then cased over with crystal. Following this procedure any colour or shape can be made. 14 cm (5½ in) high

256 Another example of a simple design on a basic shape, bought from Richardson's after their glasshouse closure c. 1925. One of a pair but obviously commercial. 24.8 cm (9¾ in) high

257 A cased blue over white vase, which could have been cameo instead of intaglio. (Intaglio is, in the glass trade, a decoration, as well as being 'opposite' to cameo.) From a set of 3 engraved by G. Woodall. c. 1923. 20.3 cm (8 in) high

258 About 1930 Stevens & Williams made a type of glassware called 'Cheane', which was either greed or red, impregnated with fine silver flecks. In some specimens the flecks formed a pattern. **258** shows it being used to case ruby with an added decoration of 'knocked in' sides. 15.2 cm (6 in) high

259 A note to collectors concerning this type of brandy flask made by Richardson's for a fairly long period both before and after 1900. No mistake should be made in identification. I know of only 2 colour combinations, firstly, red, white and blue, and secondly red, white and green, in Nailsea style. The pontil is always ground in a very untidy manner. 15.2 cm (6 in) high

260 An excellent example of a wine made especially for hock, a little above average in quality. Most have crystal stems and feet, but the bowls were made and decorated in every conceivable way – single-coloured, cased, sometimes with 3 colours, decorated with cutting, intaglio engraved, and very often cameo. The production covered many years, c. 1870–1910, probably because of the German glassmaker immigrants whose drink was hock. They were made all over England, but particularly in the Midlands. Anyone who has collected these wines is most fortunate. 18.4 cm (7¼ in) high

261 A well-designed jug made by Richardson's c. 1900, comprising thread and pinch-work, engraving and pellets. 17.8 cm (7 in) high

262 & 263 No doubt Richardson's were inspired by Stevens & Williams's 'Jewel-ware', 1886. Although for design, not in the 'Jewel' class, Richardson's used more lead in the mixture. c. 1890. **262**: 19.7 cm (7¾ in) diameter, **263**: 15.2 cm (6 in) high

264 This specimen is pseudo-cameo, and not a very imposing article, but a lot of thought has gone into its making. It is cased, speckled brown over crystal, the crystal having been worked over with a blue pattern previously. The tulip pattern has been acid-etched from the brown casing and outlined with white enamel. This was yet another attempt to produce a cheap cameo, and whenever possible, should be collected. The date is c. 1890, but I cannot hazard a guess who the makers were, other than it must have been a Midlands firm. 17.2 cm (6¾ in) high

265 A Richardson crystal cased ruby, whisky jug, the stopper being a measure. They were decorated in other patterns. c. 1910. 15.2 cm (6 in) high

266 A Richardson vitrified tazza, relying on shape for elegance. This is noticeable in all their glassware, decoration was kept to a minimum. 12.7 cm (5 in) diameter

267 & 268 A sugar and cream made by Stevens & Williams a few years after World War II. It is recorded as 'Abbey' ware and was one way of using up spare colours. The sugar's foot is unusual for the Stourbridge area, for they generally have stems. Sugar: 11.4 cm (4½ in) diameter

269 Richardson's made some gorgeous art pieces, and some unusual ones. This is not a jar but a vase. Blue was the most popular, but they were made in other colours. A shape before its time. Before 1900. 17.2 cm (6¾ in) high

270 Richardson's were noted for their tulip ornaments. This, one of a pair, is also of a series. The flowers have all the same colour combinations, but over the series a tulip bud is opening. The first one is closed, followed by the bud illustrated and so on until the flower petals are folded back. Typically Victorian, c. 1900. 17.8 cm (7 in) high

271 This is an opalescent crocodile made at Richardson's with hand moulds. The body is moulded, but the tail is pulled out whilst hot. Only intended as ornaments, c. 1890. The mould was purchased by Thomas Webb, c. 1935. 14.6 cm (5¾ in) long

272　　　　273　　　　　274　　　　　　275　　　　　　276　　　277　　　278

279　　　　　　280　　　　　　281　　　　　　282　　　　　　283

284　　　　　　　　　　285　　　　　　　　　　286

272 One of a pair of cased vases, brown over white with intaglio decoration. In this illustration the reader can see the difference between intaglio and engraving. Intaglio must have a pattern which can be cut with a large diameter stone, for speed. Stevens & Williams, c. 1910. 15.2 cm (6 in) high

273 Throughout the Victorian period candlesticks were made in vast numbers of unlimited shapes, sizes and colours in almost every glassworks in England. Stevens & Williams, c. 1918. 12.1 cm (4¾ in) diameter

274 Another specimen candlestick from Stevens & Williams, c. 1914. Candlesticks are good to collect because they can still be found in fair numbers. 10.2 cm (4 in) high

275 An example of 'Mirror Glass', silvered on Eau-de-Nil glass (Water of the Nile). Made at Edinburgh Crystal Glass Co. Ltd., silvered at Duroglass Ltd., London 1934–6, both were factories of Webbs Crystal Glass Co. Ltd. This is a similar glassware to Varnish & Co., London 1849. 22.2 cm (8¾ in) diameter

276 This is a cased example of Rockingham over citron over white. A most unusual crystal foot. Stevens & Williams, c. 1900. Note the similarity to 277. 10.2 cm (4 in) high

277 An opal, egg-body vase, on a crystal foot. Made at Stevens & Williams, c. 1900. 9.5 cm (3¾ in) high

278 Towards the end of the 19th century glassmakers tried to imitate other materials. China and silverware were quite common subjects. But this specimen imitates stone. It is exceedingly heavy, and where the punty has been, the area looks like broken marble. Thomas Webb, before 1900. 7.6 cm (3 in) diameter

279 A pot-pourri jar in Rockingham colour with intaglio design, signed RD 94025. 1888. After this date, Rockingham colour played a very important part in the Stourbridge art pieces. 14 cm (5½ in) high

280 To get this effect on a self-coloured article, a specialist, generally an enameller, was needed, but with the interest in casing, in c. 1850, the technique became simple. All the glass-blower had to do was to mark, with some pressure, the outer casing with a sharp piece of metal before the article was blown to correct size. The final blowing split the outer casing only where there were indentations.

The manufacturers of any specimen with this surface decoration are very difficult to identify. Collectors must look for other characteristics, such as, in this case the rim formation. A number of tops shaped like this one have been illustrated and they are all Thomas Webb's. The vase itself which is cased, opal over ruby over crystal, has to come from a first-class firm. Add to this a polished pontil, and we cannot be wrong. c. 1900. 14 cm (5½ in) high

281 This must be a special piece. Made by Stevens & Williams, signed and dated with their late trademark, which is after 1926. No reference can be found to it in their records. It is cased crystal over deep citron over a weak opal. The decoration (autumn leaves) has been engraved or etched on the citron casing only, which means at the citron stage the vase was cold, decorated then re-heated and cased in crystal. The black insects were painted on the outside after the vase was finished. I cannot explain the autumn leaves! 20.3 cm (8 in) high

282 This, like 280, is another example of cracked surface decoration, but so elaborate that I hesitate to name the manufacturer. The bowl is cased opal over crystal, the opal casing having rough powdered opal marvered on to the surface; colour is added and worked in from the top. The cracked surface is made exactly as for 280. Skill and ornamentation denotes Thomas Webb but colour and the type of pinch-work is Stevens & Williams. The date seems c. 1920 but the lead crystal is weak. I think it must be Stevens & Williams.

I expect most readers know that the pinched crystal band around the bowl is there to rest the bowl on a metal frame so that it could be suspended, perhaps as one of a pair, and used as a table-piece. 22.9 cm (9 in) diameter

283 Stevens & Williams gold iridescent was very popular and had 2 good production runs in 1900 and 1921. It may be a coincidence, but John Northwood I and II were designers at that time, and the colour is very similar to a type made by Harry Northwood in the United States. 13.3 cm (5¼ in) diameter

284 This is an example of Thomas Webb's soda-lime series 1900, with a more elaborate design of the Cairngoram-drops. These have blue eyes in yellow opalescent. 17.8 cm (7 in) diameter

285 Another example of cracked surface, but no mystery who made it. Stevens & Williams, in 4 colours, recorded as 'Arboresque' in 1930. Crystal over cracked iridescent surface. 27.9 cm (11 in) diameter

286 Like 196 acid-etched, but not of the same quality. The design, and coloured splotches are on the inside of the bowl, a trifle ridiculous, but I suppose it was to show skill. There is some gilding on the outside and it is very neatly applied. The bowl is Thomas Webb, c. 1900. 19.1 cm (7½ in) diameter

287 A vase of exceptional beauty, without any decoration. It depends entirely on its shape (which at first seems extravagant, but is in fact elegant) for its appeal. The glass mixture is a translucent opal, very rare, even in the Victorian period. It has a welted top and a double foot. Made at Thomas Hawkes, Dudley Glassworks before 1850. 26 cm (10¼ in) high

288 It was generally accepted that Richardson's never made thin cheap-looking glassware, but during my collecting days I have very often proved this wrong. The specimen illustrated is not rubbish, but too much time has been spent on the decoration. I saw a batch of these vases, and some were almost transparent. 1920. 30.5 cm (12 in) high

289 This vase is included for collectors to see an old-style Victorian foot. It was used extensively on early Birmingham speci-mens, but this one, cased yellow-green over white, is obviously from Thomas Webb. Two outstanding characteristics are the style of early pinch-work and the corru-gated folded top (which appears very yellow), added to clear and perfect casings. c. 1890. 19.1 cm (7½ in) high

290 Enamelling and gold work of this type is found time and time again in the Stourbridge area and it must be the work of Pierre Erard, at Stevens & Williams, c. 1890. I would not have been surprised if that evasive trademark, E over a spider's web, had been on its nicely polished pontil-mark. 15.2 cm (6 in) high

291 A fruit bowl with an exterior pattern completely threaded. The glass mixture is 'Dragon's Blood'. Made by Stevens & Williams, c. 1890. 12.7 cm (5 in) diameter

292 One of a number of wines made between the wars by Stevens & Williams. The shaped stem (formed from 9 knops) and welted foot are in their Cairngorm mixture. 19.1 cm (7½ in) high

293 A Stevens & Williams 'Regal' flower vase, c. 1945. 20.3 cm (8 in) high

294 A ruby and green, crystal-threaded vase made by Stevens & Williams before 1900. 19.7 cm (7¾ in) high

295 Another example of Stevens & Williams bubble glass cased green over crystal with moulded bubbles, 3 crystal feet, a commercial piece, c. 1945. 19.1 cm (7½ in) diameter

296 A ruby bowl with applied crystal acanthus leaves. This specimen is a type which could have been made at any one of the Stourbridge glassworks. The colour is rather weak, but it is a good commercial piece. The top and leaf formation suggest Stevens & Williams, c. 1900. 17.8 cm (7 in) high

297, 299 & 303 Although a subject in their own right, paperweights are definitely part of the Victorian period and must be discussed where relevant. Millefiore (canes) weights have been the speciality of Whitefriars, London, since 1840. The Birmingham region, however, produced more than the rest of England's output. Some were good, others little more than glorified marbles. Most date from 1850 to 1900 although J. Walsh, Walsh, Lodge Road continued until 1914. The Northern region made its own version of paper-weights, enclosing ceramic dogs, cats, fish, etc., from north Staffordshire; called 'Dumps', they were, I believe, much earlier, before 1800.

The Stourbridge area has achieved a reputation for paperweights, which person-ally I do not think it deserves. A few of exceptional beauty were made by in-dividuals to prove their ability but they were not encouraged by their masters. Stevens & Williams, I understand, ex-perimented commercially for a time. Thomas Webb have for many years pro-duced a type with bubbles as the decor-ation, nicely made but not collectors' pieces. They did however produce a few specials, fish and mermaid weights, ab-solutely superb. In c. 1932 two Czechoslovak paperweight makers came to Stourbridge to instruct both Stevens & Williams and Thomas Webb glass-blowers, but very little progress was made. The Czech workers stayed a few years working on their own. **297** was made at Stevens & Williams. **299 & 303** were made at Thomas Webb.

298 A Stourbridge walking stick, red, white and blue cane, cased crystal. They come in all colours and lengths, but are difficult to exhibit. c. 1900. 66 cm (26 in) long

300 A crystal jug with rainbow decor-ation, made at most glassworks, and a nice addition to any collection. 1910. 14.6 cm (5¾ in) high

301 An elaborate ornament, ruby cased crystal with opalescent ribs. Stourbridge made, but manufacture proved difficult. c. 1900. 19.7 cm (7¾ in) long

302 A typical Stourbridge pipe, splashed ruby over opal. These were made in all sizes and colours 15–90 cm (6–36 in) in length, but invariably opaque. c. 1900. 55.9 cm (22 in) long

304   305   306   307

308   309   310   311   312

313   314   315   316   317

These 9 specimens (304–312) are examples of that regal glassware Webb's 'Bronze'. I first read about this type of glass in Thomas Webb's record book dated 1878, but it must have been made prior to that date because in 1878 green 'Bronze', crackled 'Bronze' and 'Bronze' gilt were being produced. This of course indicates development, and generally improvements are made in styles as the development proceeds, but in my view there can be no improvement on the old Greek and Roman shapes, made in iridescent green 'Bronze' without any decoration whatsoever. I have seen pieces elaborately gilded and enamelled and also some of the shapes shown in red and blue, but I have only seen the coloured ones in glassworkers' homes, which suggests that they were not made in quantity.

I feel sure that before production ceased, 2 distinct types had developed. One followed the original vessels as near as possible, and the second, after starting with a fairly authentic shape, took liberties with decorations.

304–307 These follow, to the best of my knowledge, the true article in shape, thickness and weight, being in some cases 13 mm ($\frac{1}{2}$ in) thick and rugged. **304:** 19.1 cm ($7\frac{1}{2}$ in) high, **305:** 26 cm ($10\frac{1}{4}$ in) high, **306:** 21.6 cm ($8\frac{1}{2}$ in) high, **307:** 17.2 cm ($6\frac{3}{4}$ in) high

308 This has an owl's head for design with enamel and gilt decoration. It is pretty but hardly authentic. c. 1890. 17.8 cm (7 in) high

309 A reasonable shape, but very thin. c. 1900. 18.4 cm ($7\frac{1}{4}$ in) high

310 A splendid example of glass-making. I cannot see such elaborate articles as this being made by the Romans or Greeks. Notice Webb's shell pattern decoration, claw feet and handles on an elaborately moulded body. c. 1900. 17.2 cm ($6\frac{3}{4}$ in) high

311 The decoration on this vase is more truly Roman, but too precise. c. 1900. 12.7 cm (5 in) high

312 A much better example of a period-vase, but still too precise. c. 1900. 13.3 cm ($5\frac{1}{4}$ in) high

313 This is an example of 'Brain' glass made by Richardson's. See **315**. c. 1900. 12.1 cm ($4\frac{3}{4}$ in) high

314 What is not generally known is that cased machine-pressed glassware was made by few glassworks in the Northern region. I believe the example shown was made by Sowerby in 1882. This is a calculated guess, but I have seen this pattern, or part of it, on many signed pieces, and the company was making and advertising cased 'Slag' in 1882. See page 29. 24.1 cm ($9\frac{1}{2}$ in) high

315 One of a pair of bronze vases which could be controversial. Originally bought from Richardson's around 1900, I purchased them some 25 years ago. In 1878 Thomas Webb had produced an iridescent type of glassware which is now well-known as Webb's 'Bronze', but it is certain that Richardson's produced an almost identical type a few years later. Old employees told me that only a limited amount was produced, it being discontinued because fumes generated during the making, created a health problem.

With no records available, I can only judge from my own specimens, which I have compared with some made by Thomas Webb. I find a great difference between the 2 surfaces. The surface of the Richardson glass in my opinion resembles brain tissues, so I have always called it 'Brain' glass. As far as I can ascertain Richardson's did not make any bronze-ware, imitating Greek or Roman articles. 36.2 cm ($14\frac{1}{4}$ in) high

316 During the early 1920s old glassworkers told me that matt-finished iridescent glass could not be made. The example shown, one of a pair made at Richardson's, proved that it could. The style and finish seem to suggest it is a commercial piece. The base shows so much wear that it must be before 1900. 26.7 cm ($10\frac{1}{2}$ in) high

317 In the mid-Victorian period, Venetian glass manufacturers sold batches (glass mixtures) to many English glassworks. This was in the form of discs or short bars, the most popular being glass containing aventurine (gold fleck). Some of this was tried out in Stourbridge, but with little success. The trouble was that during the melting and making, the flecks collected in patches instead of remaining in suspense, and there seemed little they could do to prevent this. The illustration shows a small jug, which was made for a wager, proving that it could be done, and there could be others. c. 1890. 17.8 cm (7 in) high

318   319   320   321   322

323   324   325   326   327

328   329   330   331   332

318–321 Four examples of rare glassware are shown together for the decoration to be observed and compared. All are signed, 'Varnish & Co. London, Patent', on a metal disc 13–25 mm ($\frac{1}{2}$–1 in) in diameter and this is sealed into the bases. Unfortunately the most scarce of colours, yellow is not shown. Green is the common colour but all are extremely valuable and worth collecting. The 3 coloured examples, ruby, green and blue cased over crystal are decorated with cutting, whilst the last is engraved crystal.

To help the collector with this glassware, I will detail the most important points to recognize. In the first place, the signed disc in the base must be sealed and airtight, otherwise the silver deposit inside deteriorates and the article is spoilt. On English pieces, 3 names are found, all of equal importance; Varnish & Co., Hale Thomson, and W. Lund all of London. All are heavy for their size. Thousands of pieces came from the Continent, but all I have examined are light in weight, and although attractive, are worth very little. Signed American pieces are good, but still do not compare for price. From the decoration point of view, engraved pieces are by far the most desirable.

Four years covered the production of this glass. Registered in 1849 and exhibited at the Great Exhibition 1851, it was discontinued in 1852. A possible explanation is suggested on page 45. **318:** 7.6 cm (3 in) high, **319:** 17.8 cm (7 in) high, **320:** 23.5 cm (9$\frac{1}{4}$ in) high, **321:** 22.9 cm (9 in) high

322 Another example made at the Bermondsey Glass Works, London c. 1900. As with the specimen, **155**, it is signed and registered 'Applied Art' London. The piece is not what one would call a 'work of art' but as the 2 pieces shown are so different, especially their method of manufacture, there must be some exceptional specimens waiting to be discovered. 17.2 cm (6$\frac{3}{4}$ in) high

323 So called 'black' glass has never been a continuous selling line. Manufacturing friends of mine say jokingly that its sale only follows national disasters. This bowl made by Stevens & Williams in c. 1930 tried to work coloured flowers into the glass, but this did very little to improve sales. However, this glassware should be collected. 29.2 cm (11$\frac{1}{2}$ in) diameter

324 A typical English shape in black glass. Stevens & Williams, c. 1930. 30.5 cm (12 in) high

325 One of a pair of black vases with a small amount of gilt decoration. They were highly prized by Richardson's who frequently loaned them to exhibitions at the very end of the 19th century. Collectors should note the shape of foot, it is thick and heavy and was used frequently on their early glassware. 23.5 cm (9$\frac{1}{4}$ in) high

326 As explained on page 45, Whitefriars, London, encouraged artists to make their own designs. This is an example produced in the inter-war years of crystal and black glassware. 21.6 cm (8$\frac{1}{2}$ in) high

327 A fairly common type of glassware, all signed D. G. Stourbridge (the trademark is shown on page 125). The idea was to insert pictures between glass casings. Generally, these are, in my opinion, not worth collecting, but Mr. Guest the patentee, made some pictures from feathers and these I think should be collected. I have been told that some very beautiful pictures were made from butterflies' wings. c. 1920. 18.4 cm (7$\frac{1}{4}$ in) high

328 One of a pair of black machine-pressed vases, signed Trademark J. Derbyshire & Co. Manchester. 1876 lozenge. 14.6 cm (5$\frac{3}{4}$ in) high

329 An unsigned basket, but there is little doubt that it is Sowerby's, 1882. I have seen a number of these pieces in the Midlands, and all have had the outside renovated with black paint. A senseless action! 15.2 cm (6 in) long

330 One of Sowerby's vases or spills (jet). Signed 'Trademark and 1876 Lozenge'. 8.9 cm (3$\frac{1}{2}$ in) high

331 Another one of Sowerby's baskets, signed 'Trademark and 1877 Lozenge'. 8.9 cm (3$\frac{1}{2}$ in) long

332 Thought by Sowerby's to be one of their earliest machine-pressed vases (jet), signed 1852, with lozenge, it was found at the works during alterations before World War II. In 1860 a larger specimen, 20.3 cm (8 in) high was produced. 15.2 cm (6 in) high

333   334   335   336   337

338   339   340   341   342

343   344   345   346   347

There is an unfounded belief amongst glass collectors that free-blown coloured specimens worthy of collecting were not produced in the Northern region. This, of course, is not true. What is true is that a fair number of firms were established solely to produce machine-pressed goods for a cheap market both at home and abroad. The glass manufacturers south of Manchester were established for a market accustomed to free-blown goods, it was, therefore, reasonable for the Manchester area, being midway, to have a foot in each camp, and produce specimens of both kinds, fit for any collection. Although both types of goods are glassware, they are, from the manufacturing point of view, not really compatible.

333 During the Victorian period, epergnes were produced in England by the thousand. Most of the specimens made in the Midlands and South were very attractive. As flower holders for which they were intended, they were useless because they were much too fragile. The Northern ones, however, were attractive and functional. Readers should notice that the one illustrated is substantially made. Note also the flower formation which is extensively made in the Northern region. This type was made and advertised by Burtles, Tate & Co., Manchester. c. 1893. 20.3 cm (8 in) high

334 A free-blown vase, RD 21328 = 1885, made by Burtles, Tate & Co., Manchester. The collector should note that the English single flower and the American pulpit vase each have one side of the top flange turned vertically. In this specimen one side is up and the other down, a characteristic common in the Northern region. The colour, blue opalescent, is rarely found in other regions. 27.9 cm (11 in) high

335 & 336 These are examples of bellows used to show the development of the Nailsea pattern. Made by Robinson & Co. Ltd., Warrington, c. 1900. More about the Nailsea pattern on page 36. **335:** 36.2 cm (14¼ in) high, **336:** 25.4 cm (10 in) high

337 This is an example of Sowerby's free-blown 'Venetian' glassware. Many glassworks registered a Venetian-type glass periodically, and the custom has proved very misleading to collectors. In my own case I have never been able to identify any of the types by looks. Take this example, a wonderfully designed and well-made jug, yet where are the Venetian characteristics? c. 1880. 15.2 cm (6 in) high

338 Over the years George Davidson & Co. Gateshead, produced their 'slag' in opaque and translucent articles. I have used the word slag instead of malachite because, although wrongly used, most collectors themselves use the word. This specimen with trademark and RD 817751 = 1937 is obviously tableware, but nevertheless, worth collecting. 16.5 cm (6½ in) long

339 One of a pair of fireplace ornaments. It's almost impossible to name the maker as they were made at most bottle glassworks throughout the Victorian period. A single one is easy to come by, but a pair, unbroken, is most unusual. 16.5 cm (6½ in) long

340 This specimen highlights a situation which is much too common with machine-pressed glass. Here we have a treasure beautifully designed, and skilfully produced yet unsigned. It is made in 3 pieces. The base is off-white, I might suggest, to represent ermine. It had to be made at a first-class firm because of the tooling required to do the job. I can only guess at the makers, but it has many of the characteristics of H. Greener & Co., Sunderland. The shape of the crown should give me the date, but even that evades me. 22.9 cm (9 in) high

341 One of the Burtles, Tate well-known pressed swans, signed RD 20086 = 1885. Made in other sizes and colours. 12.7 cm (5 in) long

342 A machine-pressed green over white cased slag vase. Signed with the Sowerby trademark and lozenge, 1877. The specimen is ground on top which indicates that the vase was cased before being shaped (pressed). A choice addition to any collection. 7 cm (2¾ in) high

343 This is a good example of a fish posy bowl made by Molineaux Webb, Manchester, signed RD 29781 = 1885. Machine-pressed, white opalescent specimens are not plentiful so if this colour is discovered, it deserves attention. 25.4 cm (10 in) long

344 An ordinary-looking wine with some interesting features. Notice it is free-blown with a blown foot, (see page 37). On the ground pontil, H. Greener, Sunderland trademark is engraved, a practice I have never seen before. The monogram is impressed and gilded. Methods of manufacture put the date c. 1880. 13.3 cm (5¼ in) high

345 A Sowerby cake dish. I believe only 2 designs were made, but in many colours, and all are in 2 parts. The base (legs) I have seen sold many times as fruit dishes. (See page 37.) 20.3 cm (8 in) diameter

346 Another example showing the Northern region's development of the Nailsea pattern. c. 1900. 13.3 cm (5¼ in) high

347 One of a pair of vases made, I think, in the Manchester area. There comes a time when a collector, however confident, is not sure. For many years I have examined these, but cannot fault them. The metal is a bit stoney, flowers are correct formation, leaves are made and applied the right way for 1890. Blown in a mould, which should leave them a little misshapen, and they are. But I still have my doubts. 9.5 cm (3¾ in) high

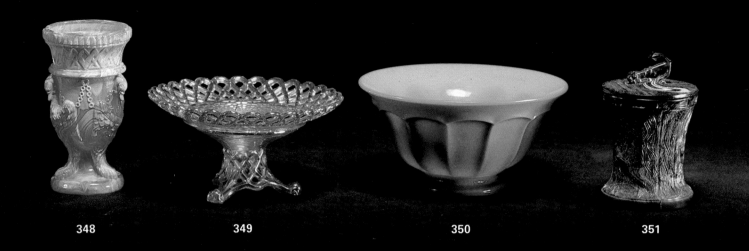

348 349 350 351

352 353 354 355 356

357 358 359 360 361

348 The annoying fact when collecting old glass is the frequent lack of officially recorded identification, but to serious collectors this should only spur them on. After all, every specimen has, in its make up, something to show its provenance.

Our first test is a blue slag vase, and unless it was designed deliberately to deceive, is Sowerby's, made before 1800. The bar pattern on the rim was used by a number of designers, but the chain and bird motif is proof enough. 16.8 cm (6⅝ in) high

349 A similar cake dish probably from the same mould, but in ruby, is shown in **345**. Here I must ask the reader to be a little sceptical about my next statement. I have always referred to this colour as Sowerby's carnival, but before 1800 the firm was advertising articles in a gold colour. All examples in my collection have been tested, and although the shades vary, they are all surface applied, which in my opinion makes them carnival. 20.3 cm (8 in) diameter

350 An unsigned Davidson's translucent bowl. In 1910 and 1937 Thomas Davidson was experimenting with this type of glassware, so there is some doubt about the date, but I think it must be the 1937 issue, because it was primarily for kitchen use. 22.9 cm (9 in) diameter

351 I have tried not to illustrate unsigned specimens unless they have some collecting interest, and I think this tobacco jar comes under that category. It could have been designed at Newcastle or Sunderland, because of its nautical nature, but my guess is H. Greener, Sunderland. Early designs from this firm tend to have small motifs covering the surfaces, and of course, we have the anchor handle. 15.9 cm (6¼ in) high

352 This dog is an example of a series of machine-pressed animals made by J. Derbyshire & Co., Manchester, signed with trademark and lozenge dated 1874. Although I have never seen any in opaque colours, they may have been made. 18.4 cm (7¼ in) long

353 Britannia from J. Derbyshire & Co., Manchester. Signed and dated as for **352**, both have the bar pattern on the base, almost a trademark for this firm. These I have seen in opaque and translucent colours, but personally I think colour cheapens them. 19.7 cm (7¾ in) high

354 Yet another specimen (goblet) from J. Derbyshire & Co., Manchester, lozenge dated 1872. (This goblet has a history – see page 37.) 21.9 cm (8⅝ in) high

355 This vase has J. Derbyshire & Co. trademark, but no date. The firm was established in 1856, and as this trademark is a little different, being large and spidery, the date could be before 1874, the usual date for this type of machine-pressed ware. 19.1 cm (7½ in) high

356 A G. Davidson, Gateshead, grey and white streaky vase unsigned. Being an unusual colour I researched it fairly well, I was not completely satisfied, but it seems to have been produced before 1880. It is matt-finished inside. 19.3 cm (7⅝ in) high

357 A very elegant commemorative machine-pressed butter dish. Australia's Centenary 1788–1888 RD 88120. H. Greener, Wear Flint Glass Works, Millfield, Sunderland. Registered No. on base and cover. 17.8 cm (7 in) diameter

358 This machine-pressed hen and chicks butter dish was made at Sowerby & Co., Gateshead – unsigned, the records I believe are destroyed but the moulds still exist. One way to check for authenticity is that the base and inside of the hen is bright blue. I cannot be sure of the date. 20.3 cm (8 in) long

359 Another of J. Derbyshire & Co., machine-pressed animals – the Landseer Lion, Trafalgar Square, London. Same trademark and date, 1874, as **352**. Made in at least 2 sizes and 6 colours and crystal. 18.4 cm (7¼ in) long

360 It is not often that we know the makers and the date of an article without knowing what it is. At first I thought **360** was a trinket tray for a dressing table, but when I found another example, but larger, I decided that it could only be a posy bowl. The boats seem to be more plentiful than the trays, in fact only a small percentage of the boat's keel is cut away to fit a stand. Sowerby's trademark is on each part, together with Registration RD 42947 for the boat and RD 52434 for the stand. Both dates come within 1886, with the stand being some 10 months later. 26 cm (10¼ in) long

361 A blue opalescent machine-pressed butter dish made at H. Greener Millfield, Sunderland. Some of the finest machine-pressed butter dishes I have ever seen were made by this firm. RD 262018 and 1895 on base and cover. 16.5 cm (6½ in) diameter

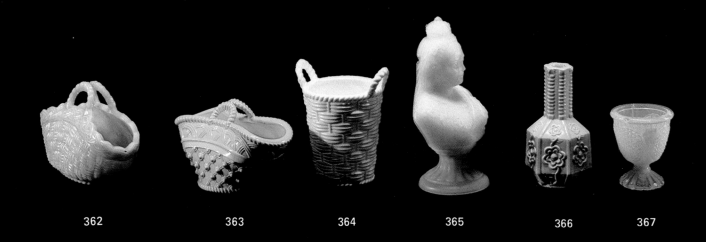

362   363   364   365   366   367

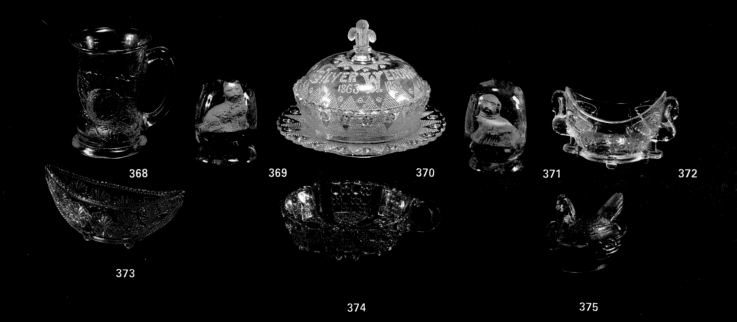

368   369   370   371   372

373

374   375

376   377   378   379   380   381

Whenever machine-pressed articles with basket-work patterns are shown for identification, Sowerby's of Gateshead must be considered, for I believe they copied every type of basket and weave used during the Victorian era.

Here are some observations which may help the collector. Notice the basket top and handles, most of this firm's basket tops were rounded, possibly fire polished. The handles which always carry the mould-joint mark have also been partly cleaned, but the pattern generally causes complications. Another interesting feature is that the baskets nearly always remain baskets without any other attachment. Also shapes and sizes conform in proportion to the true articles. Another noticeable trait concerning this range of articles is the absence of the trademark on a large number of moulds – probably to ease costs.

362–364 The first example looks like a Sowerby piece, but it does not have their finish, and the colour is doubtful as it is used by the French company 'Portieux'. **363** and **364** are both Sowerby's. c. 1876. **362**: 7.6 cm (3 in) high, **363**: 6.7 cm (2⅝ in) high, **364**: 10.2 cm (4 in) high

365 No bust of this class should be left unsigned. The detail is phenomenal, even the Queen's hair strands are perfect. The glass mixture, a translucent opal must have been carefully chosen, because of its fine satin finish. A specimen of this category could only have been made at a first-class glassworks, possibly Molineaux, Webb & Co., Manchester. The date is 1897, Diamond Jubilee year, as it is a copy of a number of portraits. 14 cm (5½ in) high

366 A blue vitro-porcelain vase, Sowerby's, signed trademark and lozenge date 1876. Notice that many of Sowerby's early specimens were ground on the top. 10.2 cm (4 in) high

367 A nice opalescent egg-cup; suggested manufacturer H. Greener, Sunderland. Perhaps one of my readers has a collection of egg-cups? These examples are not too costly. c. 1900. 6.4 cm (2½ in) high

368 A Silver Jubilee mug 1910–35 with Sowerby's trademark. 'British Made' is stamped across the base. Other than what it actually says, it might suggest that the firm had a factory outside Britain. 11.4 cm (4½ in) high

369 & 371 A pair of Northern paperweights (dumps). This kind of weight was made at John Kilner 1792–1925. The earliest weights were c. 1832. This pair was bought as Kilners c. 1890. 10.2 cm (4 in) high

370 A crystal butter dish made by H. Greener, Sunderland, RD 91449 = 1888 is marked on the base and cover, a common practice when the specimen was considered a good one. The pattern can be seen clearly, and will help to identify other pieces. 17.8 cm (7 in) diameter

372 A centre-piece from a mantelshelf set of 3. Made by Sowerby in all colours and signed, trademark, advertised before 1800. 13.3 cm (5¼ in) long

373 This machine-pressed posy trough is included to show a common pattern used by G. Davidson. RD 212684 = 1893. They come in many colours, but transparent colours are very common. 15.2 cm (6 in) long

374 A Davidson machine-pressed fruit dish, signed trademark, but not dated. Most, of this pattern, were around 1937. 12.7 cm (5 in) diameter

375 This sitting hen is shown for readers to note that while it is made from a very good mould, the glass is cheap and not finished like the Victorian specimens. As an example made in the last 20 years it may be pleasing to the eye, but it is not for a collection. 8.9 cm (3½ in) long

376 Machine-pressed shoes were made at many Northern glassworks during the Victorian period, and they actually changed patterns to match the changing fashions. They were made in all colours and crystal, and what is not generally known is that they made them in various states of repair, such as a worn-down heel or a damaged sole. A shoe mould, with slight alteration, could produce a shoe as a shoe or as a salt cellar! For the salt, the toe section is blocked off leaving an area from the back to the centre, for salt. The example shown is Sowerby's, signed, trademark and RD 87058 = 1887–8. 12.7 cm (5 in) long

377 & 378 This example is a Sowerby's machine-pressed sugar and cream, trademark and lozenge dated 1878. More about these on page 109. Sugar: 8.3 cm (3¼ in) diameter

379 Another coloured machine-pressed opalescent swan RD 20086 = 1885. Burtles, Tate & Co., Manchester. 8.9 cm (3½ in) long

380 When I first saw this shaped spill-holder, I thought it Sowerby's blue slag, but it has Davidson's trademark on the base, sharp and clear. I have always classed blue as c. 1890. 8.3 cm (3¼ in) high

381 For my comments on this pipe see its counterpart, 420. 15.2 cm (6 in) long

382   383   384   385   386

387   388   389   390   391   392

393   394   395   396   397

382 This specimen is self-coloured; it is opal vitro-porcelain, with the trade name of Blanc-de-lait (White). It is made in 2 pieces and signed with Sowerby's trademark and lozenge date 1876. 21.6 cm (8½ in) diameter

383 One of a pair of candlesticks machine-pressed by Sowerby's. On the base is the trademark, and in a 3 cm (1¼ in) diameter raised disc is the inscription 'Queen Ann Candlestick', J. Mortlock & Co., Oxford Street and Orchard Street, London. There seems some confusion about them, but obviously they were made especially for J. Mortlock & Co., in Sowerby's newly patented mixture 'Queen's Ware'. Never have I seen them dated, although every other piece of Queen's Ware I have examined is lozenge dated 1878. The colour, cream, is also consistent. I have often heard collectors say that these candlesticks were the finest examples of machine-pressed work Sowerby's ever produced. 25.4 cm (10 in) high

384 Here is another specimen which calls for some explanation. The bowl, with this size and pattern, can be found in many colours and shapes, and were made from round moulds, all shapes being formed after the moulding process but before the bowl was annealed. They have Sowerby's trademark, but no date. I judge them to be around 1880. 12.1 cm (4¾ in) high

385 This vase, one of pair, has a very distorted trademark which looks like G. Davidson's lion – the pattern is very much like theirs. It is very commercial, but the depth and crispness of the entire shape is definitely J. Derbyshire's style. The date is purely guesswork c. 1890. 17.2 cm (6¾ in) high

386 Another unsigned example, but the glass mixture is very unusual, the vase, one of a pair, looks and feels exactly like wax. Although this specimen is not marked I have found a similar vase with the rose, thistle and shamrock motif used by J. Derbyshire & Co. This example has their lion and key pattern. Date 1874. 19.1 cm (7½ in) high

387–389 These are vases from a similarly shaped mould, 3 colours are shown and there are many others. Dates could be either 1910 or 1937, the manufacturers being G. Davidson & Co. I have seen some of the black vases embossed with the words 'Made in England'. As the words had to be cut out of the mould, and were razor sharp, it suggests that the firm was eager to abide by the new law being enforced at the turn of the century. 22.2 cm (8¾ in) high

390 A jug signed with the trademark H. Greener, Millfield, Sunderland. Not dated but c. 1895. A splendid example for readers to note a pattern extensively used by this firm. The shade of blue, was also a favourite colour. 15.9 cm (6¼ in) high

391 This signed vase by H. Greener, Sunderland, shows their diversity of shapes, and also their liking for this shade of blue. c. 1895. 15.2 cm (6 in) high

392 A very unusual shape for Sowerby's, but it is signed, with trademark and lozenge dated 1884. For the collector's benefit, Sowerby's did not favour too many projections on their ornaments. 12.7 cm (5 in) high

393, 394 & 397 All are Sowerby's pieces signed with trademark, but not dated, which does not matter in this case, as all were advertised in 1880. For value it is always advisable, if possible, to buy in pairs. **393**: 11.4 cm (4½ in) long, **394**: 10.2 cm (4 in) high, **397**: 7.6 cm (3 in) diameter

395 This is a plate matching in design the cake dish **349**. They were made in a wide range of colours, and, incidentally, in another pattern. Date 1876. 21.6 cm (8½ in) diameter

396 A vase signed 'Hailware' and made by Hailwood & Ackroyd Ltd., Morley, Leeds. They made bowls and vases in vivid colours including black, but if unsigned, 'Hailware' is not worth collecting. Date 1920–30. 15.2 cm (6 in) high

398   399   400   401   402   403

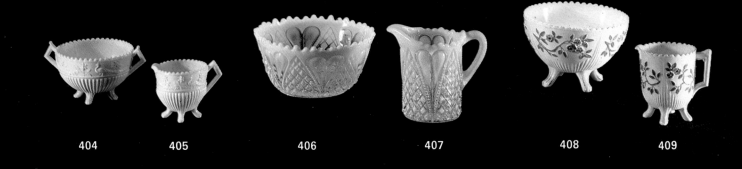

404   405   406   407   408   409

410   411   412   413   414   415

It would be very difficult to find a glass-works in England during Victorian times which did not make sugar and creams. All made different styles and shapes, some were only suitable for dolls' houses, others were large enough for the biggest family but, strange to relate, they generally remained regional.

All on this page are from the Northern region, and once again we come up against that scourge, the unsigned pieces. Although here we have a better chance of success because patterns and shapes are governed by expense, namely the cost of the mould. The use of an ultraviolet lamp has also helped me considerably. By no means is it conclusive but it does help. Luckily the majority of sugar and creams were made from an opal mixture, so if the collector will place a number of signed pieces under the lamp, he will get a visible recording as an unsigned piece is moved along. When shades coincide, it is reason-able to suppose the 2 examples are from the same works.

398 & 399 Both are signed with G. Davidson's trademark, but not the date. This date would be around 1890. The pattern is very clear for the reader to memorize, and unless there has been an exchange of moulds over the years, it must be the deciding factor. Sugar: 12.7 cm (5 in) high

400 & 401 This pair is clearly signed (on both pieces) with H. Greener's Sunderland trademark, but again not dated. The date in this case could be before 1890, although their manufacture continued for many years as the pattern is very commercial. The design is very distinct and easy to remember. Also notice the shape of the handle compared with the previous example. Sugar: 10.2 cm (4 in) high

402 & 403 A pair unsigned, but in this case there is no problem in identifying the manufacturer. The pattern, leg formation, the rustic appearance, all tell us Sowerby's, Gateshead, date 1876. Collectors must be grateful that this firm added a percentage of lead to some of their opal mixtures, giving us some chance of identification. Sugar: 8.9 cm (3½ in) high

404 & 405 These are rather small, but that does not degrade them, in fact they are the elite. They have design and shape, and are made from a mixture of vitro-porcelain which Sowerby's registered as Queen's Ware. To the best of my knowledge, all Queen's Ware pieces were signed, trade-mark and lozenge dated 1876. Note the peacock pattern, the head of which is part of Sowerby's trademark. The colour is registered as ivory, but I have formed a habit of calling it cream because I think it rather weak. Note again the pattern and feet formation. Sugar: 8.9 cm (3½ in) diameter

406 & 407 A sugar and cream made at G. Davidson's RD 413701 = 1903. This type of glassware, to me, is opalescent with a prefix which denotes colour.

A few remarks about my own experi-ences spent in the Patent Offices between the wars, may save some research workers much frustration. RD numbers officially come under the index to designs but I used them to obtain manufacturers' names and addresses. At first I thought a number denoted design, but soon found that that was not always so.

In 1891 Davidson's registered an opal-escent design and in 1903 they registered another example. In 1878 Sowerby's registered opalescent. The only difference was the colour, so you can see why I use opalescent. Sugar: 14 cm (5½ in) diameter

408 & 409 A sugar and cream made by Sowerby's, Gateshead, signed, trademark lozenge date 1879 on both pieces. Note that the design is enamelled, very few of this firm's articles were decorated in this manner, although most were ideal subjects. Sugar: 11.4 cm (4½ in) diameter

410 & 411 This sugar and cream is not marked in any way, but I have seen this pattern in crystal and it was sold as Davidson's. It reacts to ultraviolet as Sowerby's. It may even be a modern copy. Sugar: 12.7 cm (5 in) diameter

412 & 413 A sugar and cream signed only with Sowerby's trademark. As stated previously I am not sure what to call the colour. I have seen their articles advertised as gold, but I have called all my pieces carnival. The colour has been rubbed away by years of washing. The firm's gold was advertised in 1800, and these two speci-mens look that old. Not only is the colour washed away but the feet are well worn. Sugar: 12.7 cm (5 in) high

414 & 415 This pair of sugar and cream (slag) are unsigned, but I have other articles with the same colours and patterns, marked Sowerby's and dated 1887. Sugar: 11.2 cm (4⅜ in) diameter

416 417 418 419 420

421 422 423 424 425 426 427 428

416 This coal-scuttle is not signed or dated but it is an example of Sowerby's brown Malachite (slag) c.1800. The flower design is similar to that which was used on other articles. 7.6 cm (3 in) high

417 A Sowerby's signed trademark, ruby cream jug. It may be a coincidence but I have never seen a sugar to match this jug which, by the way, is fairly common. Some of the jugs were a very late issue c.1950. 10.2 cm (4 in) high

418 I have included this dish, although research is by no means complete. There are many to be found, chiefly in the Northern region, but many are so badly defaced, they are useless for collecting. This one I obtained privately and am fairly satisfied that it is not foreign. It looks exactly what one would expect to find in an early Victorian household. Surprisingly it has been made in a 4-piece mould and carefully fire polished, leaving the pattern sharp. Parts have been enamelled and finally sealed with gilt, all this work being on the back of the dish. A specimen of this type is as essential as museum pieces in any collection. 24.1 cm (9½ in) diameter

419 A green opalescent dish, very commercial, but it is important in my collection until I find a better specimen. Obviously made in the Northern region. c.1900. 11.4 cm (4½ in) diameter

420 For comparison with **381**, I will explain the details as I know them. They were both purchased in the Northern region – the blue one privately, the owners told me it was bought by an earlier member of the family at the turn of the century, when they were being sold as salt cellars, for which purpose it had continued in use. The opal one was purchased from an antique shop and bears the words 'Souvenir of Ilion, N.Y' and is surrounded with a few enamelled flowers. At first glance they both seem to be from the same mould, but the blue article is 3 mm (⅛ in) larger in all directions. This can be caused by the different contractions of different mixtures, but I think they are from 2 moulds. Although they look like pipes, the stems are solid! 15.2 cm (6 in) long

421 A satin finished machine-pressed dish made by H. Greener, Sunderland which has the lozenge date 1876. Some examples have more than one date mark, others the trademark, whilst some have both. Why, I do not know. Anyway the reader should note that there are 2 patterns, the border, and the centre 'grape' pattern.

The example shown is not, in my opinion, a good specimen to collect. I suggest that a plate is best as that is a complete article, whereas a dish is part of a service. 27.9 cm (11 in) long

422 A machine-pressed cake dish made by Molineaux, Webb & Co., Manchester with lozenge date 1864. I have had this specimen for many years, and cannot see how it could be made in one piece. Perhaps it wasn't. There is more than one size, and there are various patterns. Some free-blown and pressed articles are very similar and it is only when a pattern such as the key pattern (shown) is evident that the difference is noticeable. The Webb family, as far as I can ascertain, is not connected in any way with the Stourbridge Webbs. Another mystery remains. Did Molineaux, Webb & Co. have a trademark? 17.9 cm (7 in) high

423 Perhaps not a collector's piece for some readers, but commemorative specimens in heat-resisting glass are scarce. This example was made by British Heat Resisting Glass Co., Bilston, 1934–65. 15.2 cm (6 in) diameter

424 A splendid example of machine-pressed work, at present being researched. Signed, Director General, A. T. Coshorn. 13.7 cm (5⅜ in) long

425 As explained for **384**, Sowerby's used a round pressed bowl on 3 dolphin feet as a beginning for a number of shapes, this operation taking place before the article from the press had solidified. Many colours, both translucent and opaque were used. This example in ruby is very attractive, the piece is signed, trademark, but not dated. The production of this type of glassware is believed to be before c.1800. 21 cm (8¼ in) diameter

426 A machine-pressed goblet dated lozenge 1876, which according to the list of Registered Designs was made by J. Derbyshire & Co., Manchester. At the present time I am not wholly satisfied that it is the right firm, as part of the goblet has a Davidson pattern. 21.6 cm (8½ in) high

427 When this blue basket was offered to me, my first reaction was to refuse it. It looked modern, but a closer examination revealed the Rd 95935, which I knew to be before 1890, in fact it is 1888. The startling impression was the pattern, abstract in the extreme. Abstract to most of us means modern, yet here we have a Victorian specimen of machine-pressed glass which was commercial and, at the time, cheap. The maker turned out to be H. Greener & Co., Sunderland. 21.6 cm (8½ in) diameter

428 One of a pair of slag candlesticks without trademark or date but Sowerby's characteristics are so pronounced that we can be sure. The small leaf cascades, general design and, above all, the formation of the top all lead to that firm. The date for most of this type of ware was c.1890. 22.9 cm (9 in) high

429   430   431   432   433

434   435   436   437   438

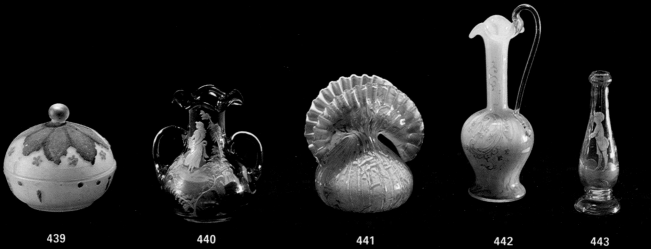

439   440   441   442   443

429 Collectors may never find an amber butter dish like the one illustrated, but might easily discover one in crystal. They were decorated (cutting) by L. & S. Hingley, Albert Glass Works, Wordsley who bought in the blanks, c. 1925. (They were made to order, and never intended as a reproduction of those made in Dublin, c. 1895.) 17.2 cm (6¾ in) diameter

430 A piece of modern Burmese – note the American pattern, althought it was purchased in Italy, 1976. 14 cm (5½ in) high

431 A specimen of Fish-Grall made at Orrefors, Sweden in 1936. It was designed by Edward Hald who experimented for years with the technique of casing any type of decoration. This is what Joseph Locke had achieved in c. 1880, but not commercially. 17.8 cm (7 in) high

432 An example of Continental applied glassware which is discussed fully on page 38. 22.9 cm (9 in) high

433 A few English glass firms used the word 'Alexandrite' to define some of their glassware, but Moser's 'Alexandrite' made at Karlsbad, Czechoslovakia in c. 1912 is, in my opinion, the nearest colour to the gem-stone of the same name. It is dichroic, but still has to be cut the right way to produce its true colour. 20.3 cm (8 in) high

434 An 18th-century German goblet, for collectors to note the pattern of engraving. See page 38. 27.3 cm (10¾ in) high

435 An example of 'Harlequin' glassware made by the Strathearn Glass Co., Crieff, Scotland. It cannot be mistaken for 'Monart' because each piece has the firm's trademark clearly raised on the pontil of each piece (see page 125). 26 cm (10¼ in) high

436 An example of cameo-revival (air-carved cameo). See page 39. 27.9 cm (11 in) high

437 This vase is Continental, and very little different from some old Birmingham ruby ones made before 1900. The only difference I can find is that the Birmingham vases had bubbles and a solid foot, whereas the Continental vases had metal flecks and a hollow foot. A crystal band 4.8 mm ($\frac{3}{16}$ in) thick has also been added. It was made on a pontil and weighs over 700 g (1½ lb). 26 cm (10¼ in) high

438 Comments on a satin jug which may not please some collectors! This is one of the few cases where almost identical articles have been produced by Continental and English glassworkers for commercial purposes. This jug is Continental and differs from the English type in a number of ways. This one has a hollow foot, the English one would be solid. Unless instructed, an English glass-blower would not pull the top too low or use this shape for the handles. To my eye the decoration is also weak and cheap! Nevertheless it is a good Continental commercial article. c. 1910–20. 25.4 cm (10 in) high

439 'Coralene' made correctly is a treasure. The American specimen, 106, shows the right size of pellets, with lustre, muffled in position (the right way of fixing). This example is Continental, very pretty, but cannot be used, and must not be handled, as the pellets will fall off. Pre-1914. 11.4 cm (4½ in) diameter

440 These vases came into England undecorated from Czechoslovakia in 1974, and were sold cheaply in stores and shops. Somewhere, someone decorated them and they were soon offered for sale in antique shops. I thought them well-designed and beautifully enamelled, and bought a pair under no illusion as to what they were, knowing that very few types of decorated glassware are repeated. 12.7 cm (5 in) high

441 An original specimen of 'Peloton' glassware first produced in Bohemia, Czechoslovakia in 1880. Without going into details it can be a shaped article, with short pieces of coloured threads partly marvered in, then cased with crystal, 104 shows an English example. 12.7 cm (5 in) high

442 A yellow, splashed white, and crystal-cased, handled vase often mistaken for early Victorian, imported into England before World War I. They come in all shapes and sizes, are fairly good quality and are worth collecting. 20.3 cm (8 in) high

443 This is a piece of authentic 'Mary Gregory' glassware from Czechoslovakia. Although only a small amount of this glassware was produced in England it must be brought into perspective. During the Victorian era it was held in great affection, and today is avidly collected.

Personally I do not know of any English firm which produced it as a cheap line. A few 'specials' and a few small orders were completed, but these were blown and pontil finished. Bohemia made both types in vast quantities. The cheaper of the two types (mould blown) is surprisingly heavy, and even when small, the thickness of the walls can be 3 mm (⅛ in).

Another point which will help the collector to select the good from the bad is the enamelling, which even on cheap Continental ware, looks 3 dimensional, and the children's clothes blend into the glass. Generally the enamelling on the English and American examples indicate curves on the figures by thickness of enamels, and do not follow the glass curvature. Regarding the American 'Mary Gregory', I do not think much of this glassware reached England, and then only from one antique dealer to another, date 1890–1914. 14.6 cm (5¾ in) high

Trademarks

A trademark has always been an elusive feature for glass collectors. Throughout the nineteenth century it was only treated seriously when it was financially helpful, or when the use was fashionable. The results show up now in many irritating ways.

In some cases a trademark was used as long as fifteen years before being registered, while others were used and never registered, the latter I have always classified as 'adopted'.

Then we find periods of intermittent use, the results of which at times are very aggravating, but here I can explain from personal experience why this often happened. If an order of two hundred vases was finished and ready for signing, (and unless it had been previously stated that *all* had to be signed) only a certain percentage would be finished in that manner, the number being governed by the importance of the order, the time available and the process used. Often only one of a pair of vases or one of a set of three was signed. These remarks apply to free-blown specimens.

In machine pressed glassware a mark is either on all, or none. If a mould has been sold to another manufacturer it is possible that the previous trademark has been removed.

A great many British glassworks started life as bottle manufacturing concerns before changing to domestic tableware, and then to producing decorative and fancy articles. Others improved their plant and kept abreast of industrial progress while many closed down.

The list of trademarks does not include bottle manufacturers unless they also produced decorative wares. Neither are they by any means complete, but they should be helpful.

London glass merchants often registered their own trademarks and claimed to be glass manufacturers, this was not strictly true but implied greater customer confidence; Vernon's Patent China and Glass Co. Ltd. (17 February 1883) is an example, but more research is needed. Judging by the number of such trademarks registered, it must have been a common sight to see these elaborate signs prominently displayed above the frontages of many 'China and Glass Merchants shops'.

Merchants often ordered goods made to their own designs and thus contributed to the production of some very collectable specimens. A case in point is the elaborate 'Queen's Ware' pressed candlesticks made by Sowerby's for Mortlock & Co., Oxford Street and Orchard Street, London, see **383**.

1792–1857, number unknown
John Kilner
Thornhill Lees
Wakefield, Yorkshire

Glass manufacturers

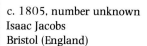

c. 1805, number unknown
Isaac Jacobs
Bristol (England)

Early 19th century? number
unknown

This 'spiderweb' is a mystery
trademark but I believe it was used
by Ensell an early 19th century
glass merchant of Stourbridge.

Established 1854 but the trademark
came much later, number
unknown

Messrs John Walsh Walsh
Soho & Vesta Glass Works
Birmingham

1867, number unknown
Abrahams & Co. (Birmingham)
Ltd. Glass Works
Gateshead, England
(was George Davidson & Co. Ltd.
until 1966)

Glass manufacturers

1869, number unknown
Bolton Son & Robinson
Mersey Flint Glass Works
Bank Quay, Warrington

EMPRESS

Established 1897, trademarks
many and varied, numbers
unknown

Webb–Corbett
Coalbournhill Glass Works
Amblecote, Stourbridge

Glass manufacturers

August 1875, No. 27,787
William Thomas Sugg
Vincent Works
Vincent Street, Westminster

ALBATRINE

6 January 1876 but in use fifteen
years before this date, No. 687
Alexander & Austin
Victoria Wharf, Earl Street
Blackfriars, London

Glass bottle manufacturers

Applied for 18 January 1876 but in
use fourteen years before this date,
No. 1012
Samuel Clarke
110 Albany Street
Regents Park, London

Patent Pyramid Night-light
manufacturers

Applied for 26 January 1876 and
not used before that date, No. 1265
John Sowerby
Ellison Flint Glass Works
Gateshead-on-Tyne

Glass manufacturer

Applied for 29 January 1876 but in
use fourteen months before
4 February 1876, No. 2982

Henry Brooks & Co.
70 Bishopsgate Street, London

Glass manufacturers
Also: Brooks–Robinson
Melbourne, Australia

Applied for 1 April 1876 and not
used until granted, No. 4464

Benjamin Lumsden Thomson
Ingram Court
Fenchurch Street, London

Decorative enamel factors

16 February 1876, No. 2261

Alphonse Morel Lodelinsart
Nr Charleroi, Belgium

Glass manufacturers

Applied for 27 April 1876 but in
use four years before this date, No.
5176

John Moncrieff
The North British Glass Works
Perth, Perthshire
North Britain
(Note the old form of postal
address)

Applied for 4 March 1876 but in
use eleven years before this date,
No. 3419

The York Glass Company Ltd.
Fishergate, York

Glass bottles

Applied for 25 May 1876, No.
5970

Elizabeth Shrewsbury & Robert
Howard
78–9 Digbeth, Birmingham

Glass manufacturers

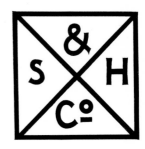

Applied for 4 March 1876 but in
use eleven years before this date,
No. 3420

The York Glass Company Ltd.
Fishergate, York

Glass bottle manufacturers

Applied for 2 September 1876 but
in use thirteen years before this
date, No. 8957

Stykes & Macvay & Co.
Albion Glass Works
Castleford, Yorkshire

Glass manufacturers

Applied for 9 March 1876 but in
use fifteen years before this date,
No. 3696

James Alexander Forrest & Son
58–60 Lime Street, Liverpool

Glass manufacturers

Applied for 29 November 1876,
No. 9851

Henry Greener
Wear Flint Glass Works
Sunderland

Glass manufacturers, all kinds

Applied for 5 March 1877, No.
11,031

Lloyd & Summerfield
Park Glass Works
Birmingham

Glass manufacturers, all kinds

Granted 5 October 1881 but in use
since 1875, number unknown

Wood Brothers & Co.
Borough Glass Works
Barnsley, Yorkshire
They also traded from:
31 Hatton Gardens
Middlesex

March 1877, No. 11,235

George Taylor & Co.
23 Seel Street, Liverpool

Glass bottle manufacturers

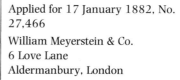

Applied for 15 December 1881 but
in use eighteen years before this
date, No. 27,249

Smith & Chamberlain
Solar Works
New Bartholomew Street,
Birmingham

Manufacturers of chandeliers &
lustres

February 1880, No. 21,918

J. Mortlock & Co.
Oxford Street, London

Applied for 17 January 1882, No.
27,466

William Meyerstein & Co.
6 Love Lane
Aldermanbury, London

Glass merchants of all kinds of glass

Applied for 22 October 1880 (in
the name of Albert Marius Silber),
No. 25,089

Silber & Flemings
56 Wood Street
Cheapside, London

Glass manufacturers & merchants

Applied for 22 January 1883, No.
31,217

S. & C. Bishop & Co.
St. Helens, Lancashire

Glass manufacturers

June 1881, No. 26,337

Dan Rylands
Atlas Glass Works
Stairfoot, Nr Barnsley
Also 'Hope' Glass Works
Barnsley

Glass bottle manufacturers

XL
Dan Rylands
Barnsley

17 February 1883, No. 31,452

Vernons Patent China & Glass Co.
Ltd.
42A Holborn Viaduct, London

China & glass merchants

Applied for 9 October 1883, No. 33,834

Miles & Pullen
The Patent Crystalline Glass Works
Clerkenwell Road
London, E.C.

Manufacturers of crystalline glass

Applied for 18 October 1884, No. 40,320

Powell & Ricketts
Phoenix Glass Bottle Works
Bristol

Glass bottle manufacturers

Applied for 23 February 1884, No. 35,744

A. Goslett & Co.
26 Soho Square, London

Manufacturers of ornamental glass

November 1884, No. 41,029

Henry Edmund, Alfred Swan &
Walter Thomas Goolden
Victoria Mansions
Westminster

Glass manufacturers

VITRITE

February 1885, No. 43,035

Benjamin Edwin Foster
23 Burnley Road
Stockwell, Surrey

Decorated glass

'KRUSTALLOS'

March 1884, No. 36,286

June 1885, No. 45,771

October 1887, No. 68,346

Date and number unknown

Samuel Clarke
Albany Street, Childs Hill
Middlesex, N. London

**BURGLARS' HORROR
FAIRY
WEE-FAIRY
CRICKLITE**

Applied for 10 June 1886, No. 54,606

Stephimus Hedges
2 Vernon Chambers
Southampton Row, London, E.C.

Glass manufacturers

Applied for 21 March 1884, No. 36,300

Robert Candlish & Son
Also trading as:
The Londonderry Bottle Company
18–20 Rotherhithe Street
London, S.E.

Glass bottles & glassware
manufacturers

THREE SPOT
● ● ●
BRAND

Applied for 11 September 1886, No. 56,664

Thomas Webb & Sons Ltd.
Dennis Glass Works
Amblecote, Stourbridge

Glass manufacturers, all kinds

18 September 1886, No. 56,859
The Mount Washington Glass Co.
New Bedford
Massachusetts, U.S.A.

Glass manufacturers

Applied for 5 October 1886, No. 57,429

A. Ruch & Company
12–13 Laurence Pountney Lane, London

Glass bottle manufacturers

October 1886, No. 58,283

Stevens & Williams
Brierley Hill Glass Works
Brierley Hill

'THE TAPESTRY GLASSWARE'

20 January 1887, No. 61,162

James Hateley
Chester Street
Birmingham

Glass manufacturers

20 January 1887, No. 61,201

Samuel Clarke
Pyramid Works
Child's Hill, London, N.W.

Night-light manufacturers

'GLOW WORM'

January 1887, No. 61,343

Thomas Ferdinand Walker & Lewis
John Murray
Trading as John Walsh Walsh
Soho & Vesta Glass Works
Lodge Road, Birmingham

Glass manufacturers

Applied for 26 April 1887 but in use five years before this date, No. 64,313

The S.S. White Dental
Manufacturing Co.
Chestnut Street
Corner of Twelfth Street
Philadelphia, U.S.A.

3 January 1888, No. 71,287

Martha Eliza Norris
33 Stoke Newington Road
Middlesex. Married Woman

Applied for 3 February 1888, No. 72,365

Arthur Mortimer
17 Ely Place
Holborn Circus, London

Glass importers

Applied for 4 April 1888, No. 74,633

Julius Bernstein & Co.
103 Fenchurch Street, London, E.C.

Glass importers

28 May 1888, No. 76,620

Lockwood Brothers
Arundel Street, Sheffield

Glass manufacturers

MONKEY

June 1888, No. 77,042
Arthur Lazenby Liberty
Chesham House
Regent Street, London

Oriental warehousemen

CLUTHA

10 August 1888, No. 79,216
T. Baillie & Co.
187 Wardour Street, London

Stained-glass manufacturers

13 December 1888, No. 83,684
James Couper (Senior), William
Haden Richardson & James Couper
(Junior) traded as:
James Couper & Sons
City Glass Works
Glasgow

Glass manufacturers

17 December 1888, No. 83,859
Stuart & Sons
Red House Glass Works
Stourbridge

Glass manufacturers

26 January 1889 but in use
since 1850, No. 85,704
La Société Anonyme et Cristalleries
De Val St. Lambert
Belgium

Glass manufacturers

January 1889, No. 85,785
William Richard Pullen
9 Farringdon Road, London E.C.

Glass mosaic & stained glass

"Cryglamos"

January 1889, No. 85,868
Stuart & Sons
Red House Glass Works
Stourbridge

Glass manufacturers

ANTHEMON

5 March 1889, No. 87,357
T. & W. Farmiloe
Rochester Row
Westminster, Middlesex

Glass manufacturers

15 March 1889, No. 87,918
Thomas Webb & Sons Ltd.
Stourbridge Glass Works
Stourbridge

Glass manufacturers

19 July 1889, No. 91,686
George A. Macbeth & Co.
Pittsburgh, Alleghany
Pennsylvania, U.S.A.

Glass manufacturers

26 July 1889, No. 91,841
Cowie Brothers
Glasgow

1890, an adopted trademark not
registered
A. & F. Pears
91 Great Russell Street
Bloomsbury
Also: 71–5 Oxford Street
London and Ilesworth, Middlesex

Glass manufacturers

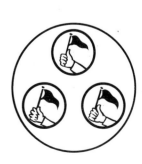

February 1891, No. 153,861

The Glass Batch Supply Co. Ltd.
19 East Cheap, London

Glass manufacturers

BUNYIP

18 November 1891, No. 160,500

Tomlinson & Co.
Manor Flint Glass Works
Stairfoot, Barnsley

Glass manufacturers

November 1892, No. 168,589

J. Dunlop Mitchell & Co.
83 Hope Street, Glasgow
Lanarkshire

'SCOTLAND, WITH ALL THY FAULTS I LOVE THEE STILL'

March 1893, No. 171,645

Newton Chambers & Co. Ltd.
Thorncliffe Iron Works
Nr Sheffield

Glass manufacturers

'IZAL'

1893, number unknown

Parker & Sanders
Birmingham

ORIGINAL. T.T.

Closed down in 1893, number unknown

J. Derbyshire & Sons
Flint Glass Manufacturers
248 City Road
Hulme, Manchester

Manufacturers of blown & pressed glass

October 1894, No. 183,231

Thomas Farrar
Standleigh
Whitefield, Manchester

Novelties in glass

'ISOBEL'

---

2 November 1894, No. 183,359

Liddle Henzell & Co. Ltd.
Ouseburn Glass Works
Newcastle-on-Tyne

Glass manufacturers
This firm had two trademarks, 'The Bulldog Brand' was probably a trade slogan.

January 1895, No. 184,792

Burtles, Tate & Co.
31 Poland Street
Ancoats, Manchester

Flint glass manufacturers

SEAFOAM

19 October 1895, No. 190,630

J. Seaton & Co.
83 Dunlop Street, Glasgow

Manufacturers of decorated glass

★AEROLITE

November 1895, No. 191,112

Arthur Pontefract
8 Grange Street
Fulford Road, York

Glass manufacture in Ebor Works

EBOR GLASS *A. Pontefract* WORKS YORK

March 1897, No. 203,406

J. Defries & Sons Ltd.
147 Houndsditch, London, E.C.

Glass manufacturers

ARBORESCENT

6 April 1897, No. 203,871

The British Lens & Glass Co. Ltd.
Coalbourn Hill, Stourbridge

Glass manufacturers

September 1899, No. 225,727

March 1902, No. 244,848

Henry G. Richardson & Sons
Wordsley Flint Glass Works
Stourbridge

ROMINTO
CEONIX

8 January 1901, No. 235,298

Charles Herbert Thompson
17 Church Street, Stourbridge

Glass manufacturer

13 July 1901, No. 239,500

Faulkner Bronze Co.
28–9 Tenby Street, Birmingham

4 October 1901, No. 241,076

Webb, Shaw & Co. Ltd.
The Dial Glass Works
Stourbridge

21 July 1902, No. 247,653

Stevens & Williams
Brierley Hill Glass Works

Decorative art-glass manufacturers

December 1902, No. 250,892

Marmart Company Ltd.
33 Old Queen Street
Westminster, London, s.w.

Dealers in painted glassware

'MARMART'

November 1903, No. 258,664

Harris & Sheldon Ltd.
Stafford Street, Birmingham

'PERMENART'

17 December 1904, No. 268,690

Poth Hille & Co.
6 Lloyds Avenue, London, E.C.

Glass manufacturers

April 1905, No. 271,905

Tiffany Furnaces
State of New Jersey
with offices at:
51 Newark Street
Hobroken (*sic*)

Glass manufacturers

FAVRILE

3 October 1905, No. 276,146

Charles Joseph Bishop & Charles
Gamble Bishop trading as:
S. & C. Bishop & Co.
29 Frazer Street
St. Helens, Lancashire

Glass manufacturers

May 1907, No. 293,207

Henry Symes & Co.
68 Bartholomews, Brighton

VERRADIANT

July 1907, No. 294,772

Willing Brothers Ltd.
49 Cannon Street, London E.C.

Glass manufacturers

ARCTIC

October 1907, No. 297,094

John Walsh Walsh
Soho & Vesta Glass Works
Lodge Road, Birmingham

Glass manufacturers

'VESTA VENETIAN'
BRITISH MANUFACTURE

17 February 1908, No. 300, 535
Charles Davis
147 New Bond Street, London

Art expert

27 July 1908, No. 305,013
W. A. Bailey & Co. Ltd.
148–150 Audrey House
Ely Place, London

Glass manufacturers

28 December 1908, No. 309,185
Arthur Kohn
1 St. Paul's Square and at
Ludgate Hill, Birmingham

Glass manufacturers

January 1909, No. 309,408

July 1910, No. 325,031
George Davidson & Co.
Teams Glass Works
Gateshead-on-Tyne

Glass manufacturers

'PRISMET'
XOL

10 February 1909, No. 310,357
Key Glassworks Ltd.
Registered Office
28 Martins Lane, London

Glass manufacturers

23 March 1910, No. 322, 051
Herbert William Taylor
Herberts Decorative Glass Works
9 New Wharf Road
Kings Cross, London, N.

Decorator

15 June 1910, No. 324,521
Dukes (Stourbridge) Ltd.
Platts Works
Platts Road
Amblecote, Stourbridge

Glass manufacturers

August 1910, No. 326,132
J. A. Phillips & Co.
Credenda Works
Bridge Street
Smethwick, Birmingham

Glass manufacturers

ENDAY

2 December 1910, No. 329,007
Lewis & Towers
Hartwell Street
Dalston Junction, London, N.E.

Glass manufacturers

February 1912, No. 340,362
Thomas Voile
37 Wellington Street, Leicester

Glass manufacturers

VIVA

23 February 1912, No. 340,560
Henry Richardson & Sons
Wordsley Glass Works
High Street, Wordsley
Nr Stourbridge

Glass manufacturers

May 1914, No. 361,510
F. & C. Osler Ltd.
230 Broad Street, Birmingham

Glass manufacturers

HELIOLITE

March 1915, No. 366, 396
Corning Glass Company
Foot of Pine Street
Corning, U.S.A.

NONEX

25 January 1916, No. 371,223
The Derby Crown Glass Co. Ltd.
Derby Crown Glass Works
Smalley Road
Chester, Derby

Glass manufacturers

May 1916, No. 372,770
United Kingdom Glass Co.
103 Wool Exchange, London, E.C.

U·K·G

May 1916, No. 373,039
Selfridge & Co. Ltd.
400 Oxford Street, London, W.

'VERTEX'

This trademark was used from
1920–1930 inclusive, number
unknown
Hailwood & Ackroyd Ltd.
Beacon Works
Morley, Leeds
Yorkshire

HAILWARE

18 November 1920, No. 153,799
Albert Harry Guest
Amblecote, Stourbridge

c. 1924, number unknown
John Moncrieff Ltd.
North British Glassworks
Perth, Scotland

Glass manufacturers

Established 1926, number
unknown
A Battersea firm of London

Gray-Stan

1926, number unknown
Stevens & Williams
North Street, Brierley Hill

1934, number unknown
British Heat-Resisting Glass Co.
Bilston

PHOENIX
MADE IN ENGLAND

May 1935, number unknown
John Jenkins & Son Ltd.
China & Glass Merchants
Holborn Viaduct
The word appears on moulded vases

'BAROLAC'

Trademarks many and varied
Thomas Webb
Dennis Glass Works
Amblecote, Stourbridge

Glass manufacturers

Webb Webb

Formerly Richardson's of Wordsley
until sold to Thomas Webb in
1930, number unknown
Thomas Webb
Dennis Glass Works
Amblecote, Stourbridge

Glass manufacturers

RICHARDSONS
BRITISH

1964, number unknown
Strathearn Glass Co.
Crieff, Scotland

Date, trademark number and
company or individuals unknown.

Index